BURN YOUR GOALS

The Counter Cultural Approach To
Achieving Your Greatest Potential

Joshua Medcalf

and

Jamie Gilbert

ISBN: 978-1-4834-1244-3 (sc)
ISBN: 978-1-4834-1243-6 (e)

Lulu Publishing Services rev. date: 06/19/2015

WARNING

DO NOT actually light your goals on fire. Fire is dangerous and can cause serious harm.

Ripping up your goals and throwing them in the trash will do just fine.

Contents

I Sleep Through The Storms

They were putting on a competition to attract the best architects and designers in the world. They told everyone that budget wasn't an issue. Send us your building proposal and we are going to choose one person or firm to get the contract.

They had their eyes on 50 or so building designers even though they received thousands of submissions from all over the world. This would be one of the most prized contracts in architectural history.

Most designers sent in proposals that were inches thick. One designer, however, sent in a fax with one sentence: "I'll sleep through the storms."

They called the designer to let him know that his assistant must have made a mistake, because all they got was the one sentence without a proposal.

He told them there was no mistake. "I sent it to you on purpose." They were confused but slightly intrigued. The designer went on to explain that he didn't know how much it would cost to build his design because he would make sure the building was built in the best way possible. He also didn't know how long it would take because during building projects unexpected events happen all the time. He also told them he wasn't interested in sending them an inflated résumé like all the other designers. He did however make them a promise: "I will sleep through the storms."

He went on to explain that when the building was finished he would never worry when the storms hit because of how well he would build the building. He told them that when the storms come they would want to call him to ensure the building would be safe. But he said, "Do NOT call me, because I sleep through the storms."

He was awarded the contract.

We teach people how to build their own lives on a firm foundation and how to live in a way that allows them to peacefully sleep through the storms that inevitably come in their life. 4 years ago I was living in the closet of a gym. 2 years ago Jamie was picking golf balls off a driving range. 3 years ago I was turned down for an entry-level job by a rental car agency. 2 years ago Jamie was denied a job to stock shelves at a grocery store. Today, we serve individually as the directors of mental training for UCLA women's basketball, and Denver Men's Golf. We have worked with people in the NFL, NBA, MLB, PGA, LPGA, MLS, Fortune 500, Forbes 30 under 30, and we the privilege of serving people in over 60 countries around the world. We created the first mental training apps in the country for basketball, golf, and soccer and our brand *Train to be CLUTCH* is one of the most sought after and respected consulting brands in the country. We are passionate about our mission and proud of our work thus far. The best part...we sleep through the storms.

Would you like to sleep peacefully through the storms?

Then let our journey begin!

The FOUNDATION Of This Work And Our Lives

We believe the strategies in this book, if applied consistently over time, can help you unleash your greatest potential. They can help you go from merely surviving to thriving, from living out of fear, to having courage to chase the lions and climb the mountains in your life. However, we believe the ultimate path to deep satisfaction and true fulfillment can only be found through Jesus. We do not expect you to believe what we believe, and even if you don't believe what we believe, we think you can find immense value from the stories, tools, and strategies within. Our hope is that you will feel encouraged, refreshed, and maybe even a little bit lighter after reading this book. We want you to know that YOU matter, and that God loves you unconditionally regardless of whether you believe that, whether you change your behavior, or whether you ever "do" anything for Him. He is crazy about you, and His love is extravagant, unconditional, undeserved and greater than anything we can ever imagine. Religion = Do. Jesus = Done.

We also believe, at a foundational level, that your value comes from who you are, and not from what you do. We believe you are infinitely priceless because of who created you, and what He says about you. We believe we have all been perfectly and meticulously created for a purpose.

Once again, you don't have to believe what we believe, but that is what we believe and we want to be crystal clear about it from the beginning! ☺

Before We Begin....

Some of the things we will talk about are going to sound crazy and many are countercultural, but we have seen them benefit people from all walks of life.

Some of our strategies might require some uncomfortable breaking down and being put back together in ways that are more beneficial.

For example, in order to get a better golf swing I had to get worse for a little bit in terms of results, so that I could develop a better swing and more sustainable golf game. It wasn't easy, and at times it was frustrating, but I'm glad I did it. After a few months of taking lessons and working at the range by myself, I was consistently shooting scores I couldn't touch with my old swing.

Sometimes in life we have to change strategies to reach our full potential. Jay Z sold drugs to help get himself out of the Marcy housing projects in Brooklyn, but he never would have become the business mogul he is today if he hadn't shifted gears and changed strategies. **Many times what got you to this level won't get you to the next level**. We see it all the time in collegiate athletics. Young people have to learn that the strategies that helped them be successful in high school sports and got them to college, will rarely help them excel at the collegiate athletics level. The same transition often happens from college to professional athletics and no doubt holds true in business across all sectors.

For us, most of this is not a matter of right and wrong. It's a question of what is most **beneficial**. We don't expect you to believe everything we believe, but we have seen some incredible results in our lives and in the lives of the people with whom we have had the pleasure of sharing this journey we call life.

We've learned that what got us to this level will rarely get us to the next level, and that the toll-way to greatness is a very costly road.

Some of the concepts and strategies we discuss are simple, but we all know simple doesn't mean easy. We learned from Chuck Noll, "Champions do ordinary things better than everyone else."

We are excited and truly grateful you have found our work! We hope you will open your heart and join us on this journey ☺

Put First Things First

When we put first things first, second things are not suppressed, rather they increase. –C.S. Lewis

For us, putting first things first is where everything should start. We put so much emphasis on winning and success in our culture, it makes us wonder if one day we will get to the top of the ladder and realize our ladder was on the wrong building.

A Journey To Putting 'First Things First'

So, I want to tell you a little bit of my journey to give you practical examples of how putting 'first things first' and not having goals has played out in my life.

Ever since I started reading John Grisham books as a 10 year-old, my dream had been to become a brilliant litigator. But then 6 years ago the entire trajectory of my life changed by asking a simple question: "What would I do if money didn't matter?"

It wasn't go to law school. In fact, it really shocked and kind of bothered me because my answer was *serve people*. You might be thinking that sounds normal enough. *BUT YOU DIDN'T KNOW ME.* When our soccer team in college would do a community service event I would complain for the whole week leading up to it, and at least 2 weeks after it, and this was after making sure I did as little as possible while at the event.

SO FOR ME, and all the people who knew me, this was a radical idea!

Then one day, I was convicted that if I would serve people if money *didn't* matter, then that was what I should do if money *did* matter.

I passed on scholarships to law school and applied to do a full time live-in internship at a massive non-profit homeless shelter and service organization in Los Angeles, California, called the Dream Center. In the 6 month interim before moving to LA, I was traveling the country and trying to run a network marketing company with a product I had been involved in at Duke. I was in different cities every few days and every time I got to a new city my friends wanted to go out.

I knew it was bad when I found myself inebriated and sleeping in a field in Lamar Missouri, with the police leaving a message on my phone asking me to turn myself in. I came home from that trip and realized I needed to make some drastic changes in my life. I drove to LA the next week not knowing if I had a felony arrest warrant out for me. Turns out the cops had lied, *shocker*. But I definitely drove the speed limit the whole way to LA.

My radical new mission for my life was to love and serve people. After doing the internship and living in the homeless shelter for 6 months, I upgraded my living conditions by moving into the *closet of a gym* to start my organization and serve as the sports director at a local church. Yes, a real closet. No windows, kitchen, bathroom, or anything of the sort. It was a large closet, but a closet nonetheless.

Now remember, all I have been doing is trying to love and serve people since I moved to Los Angeles. I had no *goals*! While still living in the closet, my dream law school, Pepperdine, asked me to give a keynote to the entire undergraduate student body and paid me more money than I'd ever been paid up to that point in my life.

Pepperdine needed someone to teach a sport psychology class, and I was asked if I would like the position. However, it ended up I couldn't teach because I didn't have a master's degree in something. After finishing all my coursework at Duke for my masters program it never felt right in my heart to write my thesis to actually get my masters. After wrestling with writing it for many months, I eventually decided I wasn't going to write the paper. Many people told me I would regret that decision for the rest of my life. After Pepperdine asked me to teach sport psychology those same people tried to rub it in my face, "I told you, you were going to regret not writing your thesis." **My response was, "I believe my father created the world, so I am sure there is a better opportunity out there for me."** Rarely do we have control over what happens to us, but we always have 100% control over how we explain what happens to us. *Many times the most important thing is not actually what happened, but how we explain the event to ourselves.* I just kept my head down and focused on loving people, serving people, and providing value.

Growing up my dream school to play at was the University of North Carolina, and the 3rd workshop I ever did with a college program was with UNC women's soccer, the greatest dynasty in college sports. At that point they had won 20 out of 29 total NCAA National Championships ever played in Women's Soccer.

Less than a year later, Cori Close, the person serving as the head coach of UCLA women's basketball, who was personally mentored by John Wooden for nine years, sent me a direct message on Twitter, and asked if she could take me to lunch.

What??? Take me to lunch?? Of course!

Now remember, all I have focused on is loving and serving people since moving to LA. *Every meeting I have gone into, I have had no agenda and no goals.*

I would simply ask people, "What is your dream? How can I help?"

As tempting as it was to go into this meeting with a goal, I stayed true to my mission and just asked my normal two questions. Cori goes on to tell me they need someone who is local to be their mental coach. ***Are you kidding me?!*** I have been telling people in coaching they need someone in this position for over a year, and here is someone at the school with more national championships than any school in the country telling me she needs one, *AND SHE WANTS ME TO DO IT?!*

All Jamie and I have focused on is putting first things first, and without sport psychology degrees, we serve as directors of mental training for some of the top college sports teams in the country. We have the great honor and privilege of mentoring and coaching some of the best in the world from all walks of life.

All I did was put first things first and I was giving a keynote at my dream law school, doing a workshop with the greatest dynasty in college sports, and serving as the director of mental training on John Wooden court every week.

When you put FIRST things FIRST, second things are not suppressed, they increase. ***I didn't have GOALS. All I tried to do was love people, serve people, provide value, and God took me places beyond my wildest dreams.***

Let's also remember:
We don't know what is possible.
We tend to chase stuff that is harmful for us.
We don't know what is realistic.

Most of the people who changed our world have been considered crazy and far from realistic.

Let's focus on identifying and putting first things first in our lives, and trust the results will take care of themselves.

One way we help people figure out what the 'first things' are in their life is to write out their obituary.

We would ask that you take 3 minutes and **ACTUALLY stop and write out** what you want to be said about you when you are gone. What do you want to be remembered for?

We've done this exercise ourselves and with people all over the world and, regardless of age, people never put down how much money they made or how many championships they won.

(I have a confession. I'm usually the guy who has trouble following directions, but this is one exercise you really want to do.)

On your deathbed it is unlikely you will wish:

You won more games.
You made more money.
You had more stuff.
You had a better title.
You got one more sale.

What it usually comes down to are our relationships and personal characteristics. These are the things we write down in our future obituary. These are the things we will care about. We will wish we loved more and spent more time with those we love. We will wish we didn't live in fear. We will wish we put 'first things first'. When we take the time to get in touch with our heart we know what those first things are, and the sooner we put them first the more peace and success we will have.

Suggestions for applying 'Put First Things First'

"Alright! I got your voicemail and I am very confused. What is your business model?!"

Jamie and I laughed on the other end of the phone, and Jamie told him we don't have a "business model." Our "business model" is love people, serve people, and provide value.

As a business we have never focused on making money, never had a business plan, or any type of business goals, and in less than 3 years we have apps in over 56 countries, have reached hundreds of thousands of people with *Train to be CLUTCH* tools, and receive between $5k and $15k for workshops and speaking engagements.

We focus on these things:
-Spending time with Jesus
-Putting hearts first
-Reading and studying wisdom
-Tweeting valuable tools to people all over the world
-Finding and writing compelling stories
-Creating valuable mp3's and videos
-Breathing life into and encouraging people and their dreams
-Sharing strategies that have helped us
-Modeling what we teach
-Sitting at the feet of mentors who have accomplished their dreams
-Being authentic
-Chasing metaphoric lions

Here are some examples of what putting 'first things first' looks like for us:
- Loving God
- Putting people's hearts first
- Loving People
- Serving People
- Providing Value
- Our Health

Here are some examples of what putting 'first things first' might look like for someone in coaching:
- Putting the hearts of those you lead above performance

- Focusing 100% of energy on the process
- Spending high quality time with family every day
- Seeking wisdom every day
- Developing the person first and foremost

Here are some examples of what putting 'first things first' might look like for a person playing sports:

- Commit to seeking wisdom every day
- Skipping parties to put in extra training
- Focus on the process rather than results
- Focus on progress rather than achievement
- Focus on developing your game vs. getting exposure
- Focus on using your sport to develop more true mental toughness rather than being used by your sport by focusing on results that are outside your control

Here are some examples of what putting 'first things first' might look like for a person in business:

- Putting people over profits
- Choosing to use every moment at work to focus on developing great communication and self-control
- Treating customers and colleagues with respect even when you don't feel like it
- Focusing on developing trust and transparency over profit and promotion
- Spending quality time with your family away from work

Burn Your Goals

*"Be faithful in the small things for it is
in them that your strength lies."*
–Mother Theresa

I want to tell you how this all started.

Last fall one of the girls I train who plays collegiate golf sent me a text message with a picture of her goals, and it was the final straw. I was tired of seeing people get high off of the thrill of setting big goals when they weren't willing to commit to controllables.

I told her, "Burn your wish list. I want to see your commitment list. I want to know what you are committed to doing with your 24 hours a day to close the gap between where you are and where you want to be. What are you willing to sacrifice inside your 86,400 seconds every day to become the person you want to be?!"

We don't have control over outcomes, but we do have control over how we use our time. **Time is the only resource that is the same for everyone regardless of how much money you make, your race, or where you live. We only get 86,400 seconds every day.**

My whole life transformed when a mentor of mine asked me a simple question over coffee. He said, **"What do you do with all your time?"**

I pontificated for the next few minutes about all the things I did with my time, but he seemed to have bought it. However, that question haunted me for the next few days.

I knew I had massive dreams, and how I used my time was not in direct proportion to the size of my dreams.

I started cutting a lot of stuff out of my life, and drastically changed what I did with my time. I was guilty, as many of us are, of running towards all the stuff that was keeping me from my dreams: Friends, chilling, Facebook, TV, staying busy, parties, and many other time wasters.

For six months I studied like a student in medical school reading for up to 15 hours a day. Most of my friends and family told me I was crazy. I had to block out a lot of noise from outside influences. *When you are climbing out of a bucket full of crabs, there will be many people who try and pull you back down to their level.*

After six months, I found myself in an elevator with Anson Dorrance along with 15 other people. Anson Dorrance serves as the head coach of the University of North Carolina Women's Soccer program. We got off the elevator and everyone turned right, Anson and I went left.

I asked him, "Who works with your girls on mental training?" He said, "I do. I can read and write!" Touché! If I had won 20 out of a total of 30 national championships ever held in my sport, I would probably be very confident in my work as well.

I asked if he knew who Barbara Fredrickson was, and he said "I do not. Why should I?"

My response sounded as fast as an auctioneer at a car auction.

"Her research on positivity shows that if your positivity ratio is around 1 to 1 that forecasts clinical depression. If your positivity ratio is around 2 to 1 that forecasts languishing in life. But if your positivity ratio is over 3 to 1 it hits this funny tipping point and it starts to forecast flourishing, regardless of how you define flourishing. It also impacts individuals and teams in a similar way. OH, and she teaches at this little school you might be familiar with, the University of North Carolina at Chapel Hill."

Slowly a huge smile spread across his face, and he stopped dead in his tracks. "Can you write that down for me? You might have just made my trip here worthwhile."

Three months later he had me out to work with his program as the third outsider ever to work with UNC Women's Soccer on mental training. I don't have a sport psychology degree, but drastically changing how I used my time got me an endorsement and relationship with one of the greatest people in coaching.

I was really frustrated for a long time because I felt like nobody took me seriously. The real problem was *I didn't take myself seriously*. When I started taking myself seriously I drastically changed how I used my time.

Make sure your willingness to sacrifice and how you use your 86,400 seconds every day are in direct proportion to the size of your dreams.

We have control over how we use our time, but we don't have control over our goals. We know it is countercultural and potentially crazy to let go of goals. It goes against everything most parents, mentors, self-help books and expensive special consultants implore us to apply. But no one sits around at the beginning of the year and says:

"Our goal is to finish last place in the conference"

"Our goal is to have the worst shooting percentage in the country"
"Our goal is to have mediocre season"
"Our goal is to get out-sold by every competitor in the business"
"Our goal is to have negative cash flow"

You never hear this!

*EVERYONE **WANTS** TO WIN. EVERYONE **WANTS** TO GROW.* Very few
are willing to do what it takes.

It is easy to have a goal setting meeting. It is hard to get up day
after day and put the work in when everyone else is having more
fun, spending time with friends, making more money, and doing a
hundred other things you would rather be doing in the moment.

**What if our *GOALS* were actually holding us back from becoming
the people we want to be and achieving our greatest potential?**

Rather than focusing on arbitrary goals, we try to focus 100% of
our energy on our commitments and controllables.

Here are some examples of controllables:
-Self-talk
-Routine
-What we do with our 86,400 seconds every day
-Perspective
-Communication
-Processes
-Visualization
-Attitude
-Focus
-Body Language
-Gratefulness

By focusing on controllables you naturally close the gap between
where you are and where you want to be.

By focusing on outcome-based goals that are outside of your control, you increase pressure, decrease confidence, and make yourself and those you lead miserable in the process.

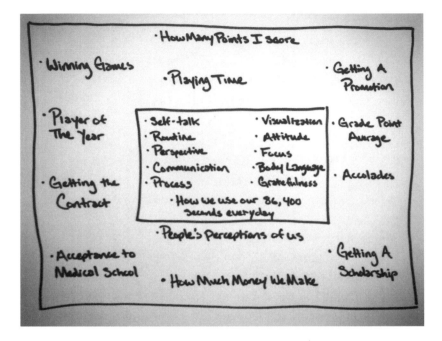

The inner box are the things we can control, the outer box has examples of things outside of our control. Focusing your energy on the outer box is a recipe for an emotional rollercoaster! If we will commit to focusing all of our energy on the inner box we will get better results and have a greater sense of peace.

We know that for many people removing goals is like taking away the training wheels, but it's long over due. In the beginning goals served a purpose, but eventually you outgrow them. At some point training wheels are more of a hindrance than a help. You can't go off cool jumps and your experience is severely limited with training wheels on.

Have you ever seen someone compete in the X-games with training wheels?!

Another Common Objection

We see the fear in many peoples' eyes when we suggest letting go of outcome-based thinking and burning their goals. We know it's a scary idea and people in leadership often tell us they *need* goals to help their team or organization have something to strive for. Holding the stick with a carrot dangling down, they ask, "What will they work towards if we don't have goals?"

Our answer: We should be working towards *True Mental Toughness*
We define True Mental Toughness as:
Having a GREAT attitude
Giving your very, very best
Treating people really, really well
Having UNCONDITIONAL gratitude
REGARDLESS of your circumstances.

Relationships and personal characteristics are what we *know* are most valuable in life. If we focus all of our energy on developing true mental toughness we can use our sport, job, relationship, and challenges to become the type of people we want to be, rather than being used by our context.

We hear it often from people in coaching, parenting, and even politics that sports are transformational. But we would argue that they are not intrinsically transformational. ***But they can be!*** Too many people are being used by their sport and are actually being conditioned to have some characteristics that are less than beneficial.

They are learning:
*It is acceptable, and sometimes encouraged, to **not** treat people well after a tough game.*
Cheating is okay as long as you don't get caught.
Their value comes from winning and losing a game.
*Getting the **W** is all that matters.*

Treating people harshly is okay as long as it leads to a positive performance.
Sacrificing relationships is worthwhile if you win.

Think about this:
Do you want to work for someone who only treats you well whenever you are performing at peak levels?
Do you want to live with someone who only has a good attitude when everything is going well in his or her life?
Do you want employees who are only grateful when you give them bonuses?
Do you want to be a part of a team that only gives it's best when individuals are playing well?

If we set arbitrary outcome-based goals for those we are leading, we are actually creating more entitled people. Much like the parent who pays his or her 10 year-old according to the points she scores, we are conditioning them to believe that there needs to be an external prize at the end of the work. If we focus on the goal, then we are setting people up for a life of, "What can I get for doing this?" rather than:
"How can I learn and grow from this?"
"How can I serve others?"
"How can I make our team better?"

Imagine the implications for relationships alone! If we are focusing on developing true mental toughness individually and collectively we are instilling value driven attitudes inside those we lead. We are telling them it is who we become on the journey NOT the prize that is most valuable. **If, and only if, we focus on true mental toughness can we take back the transformational power of sports and *USE* them to refine our character.** By focusing on True Mental Toughness all we can do is win, because if we are performing poorly it is an incredible opportunity to develop more True Mental Toughness. If we are performing well, then it's a win if we are focused on the things under our control. This same concept applies in business and other facets of our life.

But "Goals" Are Ingrained In My Vocabulary

Before we move forward, it's important to clarify what we mean by "goals." We mean things outside of your control, so mainly things that are outcome-based.

Examples would be:
- Being salesperson of the month at your company
- Making a certain amount of money in a year
- Making a certain number of sales in a set period of time
- Winning the conference championship
- Finishing Top 3 in the conference
- Making a 3.5 GPA
- Finishing Top 10 in the country
- Winning a national championship
- Getting a scholarship to play a sport in college

While there is a measure of controllable action in each of these contexts, these are all examples of ends that can be, and often are, determined by forces outside our control. Let us explain.

Winning a game is a combination of many factors, some controllable and some not. We've all seen teams or been a part of teams that have played extremely well, fought through adversity and have given every last ounce of effort only to lose because of a referee's decision, crucial injuries, or one decisive slip on the court. Though we give maximum effort and do everything in our power to win, we may still come up short. *The fundamental principle is that outcomes are outside of our control.* If we could control results then we would no doubt be the highest paid commodities in the world! But we can't.

One example of this came from my time playing soccer at Duke. We played Alabama A&M on a hot Sunday afternoon, and we were a much better team. We outshot them 19 to 6. I drew a penalty kick 7 minutes into the game, and my teammate, Mike Grella, put us up 1-0. The next 83 minutes of play was probably the craziest of my career. Alabama A&M went on to score 5 goals on 6 shots, and 4 of those goals were scored with shots to the top corner of the goal. I've never seen anything like it. Results are often outside of our control, and on that hot Sunday afternoon I learned this lesson the tough way in a 5-4 loss.

So What Do We Do?

Rather than setting arbitrary goals and focusing on the outcomes: *create a compelling mission for your life.*

You don't have to become a doctor to be able to live out the mission of serving the needs of the sick.

You don't have to win a championship to be able to live out the mission of pursuing excellence and being a beneficial role model for youth in your community.

You don't have to have a "ministry" in order to show people the love of Jesus, serve their needs, and give them hope.

Create a compelling mission for your business.

Create a mission and list out the commitments that are 100% controllable and commit to pursuing true mental toughness.

If you are selling cars, don't let numbers drive you. Realize that you have the opportunity to make a family's life more efficient and safer by finding them the most suitable car for their needs.

When people and groups commit to being mission-driven rather than goal-driven, we have seen the results take care of themselves. Oprah had this to say to the graduating class at Stanford:

I was always happy doing my talk show, but that happiness reached a depth of fulfillment and of joy that I really can't describe to you or measure when I stopped just being on TV and looking at TV as a job. I decided to use television. To use it and not have it use me. To use it as a platform to serve my viewers. That alone changed the trajectory of my success.

John Wooden said, "I've yet to meet a cynic who can describe for me what you can do beyond one's best." We believe we have raised the bar by adding the three additional tenants to True Mental Toughness. They are very challenging, but 100% controllable.

In their book, *Built To Last*, Jim Collins and Jerry Porras give many examples of how Mission-driven companies always out-perform profit-driven companies in the long run.

Companies like Apple, Sony, and Facebook have never focused on maximizing shareholder profitability; rather they have focused on their mission and have become extremely valuable as a byproduct.

When the pharmaceutical company, Merck, brought antibiotics to Japan after WWII it was not a profitable endeavor, but today Merck is the largest pharmaceutical company in Japan.

George Merck II summed up putting first things first when he said: "We try to remember that medicine is for the patient. We try to never forget that medicine is for the people. It is not for the profits. The profits follow, and if we have remembered that, they have never failed to appear. The better we have remembered it, the larger they have been."

In, *Built to Last*, Collins and Porras write, "Contrary to business school doctrine, *we did not find "maximizing shareholder wealth" or "profit maximization" as the dominant driving force or primary objective through the history of the most visionary companies.*"

Please let go of the wish list. Focus on what you are committed to doing in order to close the gap between where you are and where you want to be.

Remember, you don't have to be the C.E.O. to make a difference either. At a Jamba Juice in Highlands Ranch, CO, one of the people working there wrote "You are loved" on my drink. I don't know if this was authorized, but I can tell you it made my day, and made me want to go back there again and again!

Common Objections to Burning Your Goals

At this point many people tell us, "All of that *sounds* great, BUT THE REALITY is"
I have to win to keep my job.
I have to make money to pay the bills.
My company has sales goals I have to hit.
My coach told me I need to score 15 points and have 8 rebounds a game.
I have to reach this goal *or else!*

We have seen example after example of how focusing on True Mental Toughness, controllables, and commitments has led to drastically increased results. We aren't saying sacrifice results, we are saying let go of them and focus on what you actually have control over.

We haven't lowered the bar, we've RAISED it!

When we focus on the process, the results take care of themselves. As John Wooden said, "you may not like the results, but the results will probably be pretty close to what they should be." **By letting go of goals and focusing on commitments, controllables, and true mental toughness there's MORE accountability, because unlike outcome-based goals, our commitments are 100% inside our control.**

The Scariest Part About Goals

Regardless of whether you achieve your goals or never come close to them, they have the potential of *defining your worth as a person.* I want to be clear that we don't believe there is anything inherently wrong with winning a championship or winning the prize, but when those accomplishments make us "better than" other people or more "inherently valuable" than others, then that is where it becomes extremely problematic.

We believe our value is intrinsic and comes from being a child of God, who He meticulously and perfectly created for a purpose, and not from what we do. What we do and how much value we provide to the world might impact how much money we can make, a starting spot on the team, or result in a cooler job, but it can never change our intrinsic value as a person. Every person on earth is inherently worth the same: *Infinitely priceless.*

But is that the message our society teaches? Hardly! Watch or listen to sport shows and count how many times they talk about someone's identity and value according to their stats, accolades, or mistakes. Read popular magazines and see how often they talk about someone having "made it" because they are on TV or won an award.

What our society tells us is that our intrinsic value is attached to what we achieve or don't achieve. This is very destructive! We always ask people who play and coach whose records are not glamorous how they would carry themselves if their team was 15-0. Every single one of them nervously laughs and says, "I'd probably be feeling pretty good." Every single one of them says they would be more diligent in their process, and they would treat people better, including themselves. But the reality is that if you feel like you are nobody without it, you'll never be anybody with achieving your goal. *True satisfaction and fulfillment cannot be found through achievement.* If you want to know where we find ultimate satisfaction watch or listen to the Jesus Is _____ music project on YouTube or iTunes.

Your worth as a person is set. You are no more valuable or less valuable because of what you do! *When we focus on the process of growth and true mental toughness we steer the souls of those we impact away from the treacherous emotional rollercoaster of results-based identity and towards the journey of growth and development.*

Other Dangers Goals Create

Here is another challenge with "goal talk." If we are trying to build confidence based on accomplishments from things those we lead have done in the past, our attempts to encourage them when they are struggling with results are more apt to fall on deaf ears. If we have praised them in the past for what they achieved, then we have conditioned them to understand that the value comes from the result, not the growth, and definitely not from enjoying the journey. When they hit the inevitable plateaus on the *Path to Mastery*, those dry spots where nothing seems to get any better even with countless hours of deliberate practice, they will be more likely to relent or give up because they have been conditioned to believe the work is only worthwhile if the goal is achieved, and the outcome attained.

The beauty of sports is that the parameters of winning and losing are already defined for us, so we don't need to spend any time focused on them. We can focus all of our energy on things within our control. John Wooden said you couldn't find a person he coached who EVER heard him mention winning.

Most people who coach golf understand the importance of letting go of outcome-based thinking. They always tell the people on their team to focus on one shot at a time and not get ahead of themselves. This advice doesn't just apply to golf; it applies to all sports and all of life. If we get ahead of ourselves and are thinking about everything in the future, we detract from our ability to fully engage in the present moment. When we get ahead of ourselves, we tend to trip and fall. You see it all the time on Sundays with people who play in the NFL. A guy starts running before they secure the catch, and they end up dropping the ball, or worse, popping it up for an interception. If we focus on doing our very best in the present moment, the results will take care of themselves.

Burn Your Sales Goals As Well

A girl I used to date was working as a leasing agent for a very large property management company in California and her company always set weekly sales goals for her. She is an amazing person, and one of the best employees I've ever known. However, her goals never helped her become the number one leasing agent in the country for her company. This only happened after she burned her goals and focused all her energy on the process and her commitments. She focused on making a certain number of phone calls every day and following up with a certain number of leads everyday. She didn't have control over hitting an arbitrary sales goal, but she did have control over how many calls and follow ups she did every day. This little shift helped her go from getting good results to getting great results. It also released unnecessary stress and allowed her to fulfill her greatest potential. It is another example of how putting first things first and letting go of outcome-based thinking actually leads to better outcomes.

Dreams vs. Goals

We want to make one thing clear. There is a difference between a goal and a dream. A dream is something planted deep in your heart that has been there as long as you can remember. A goal is something you set. A dream is something you have always had in your heart.

The Opposite Of Trust

Proverbs 3:5-6 says, "Trust in the Lord with all your heart, lean not on your own understanding; in all your ways acknowledge Him, and He will direct your paths."

Most of our goals are actually selfish ambition if we are really honest. They are antithetical to Proverbs 3:5-6. We are not the architects of our lives. We are the person, flesh and blood, who has the most say about our lives, but there are many factors outside our control. And if you consider yourself a follower of Jesus, we would ask you to take a look at your goals to see if they are in opposition with Proverbs 3:5-6.

Dr. Ben Carson says that one of the most important things he learned growing up was that, "the person who has the most say about you in this world, is you." Notice he says the *person!* This leaves the necessary room for God's sovereignty while still upholding our free will to make choices. We believe God empowers us to make choices in the way we live, but when we act as though *we* know what is always best for us, we must remember the humbling words from the book of James:

Look here, you who say, "Today or tomorrow we are going to a certain town and will stay there a year. We will do business there and make a profit." How do you know what your life will be like tomorrow?

What if we missed an opportunity to love someone because we lost the national championship game and we were focused on the wrong things?

What if in the pursuit of that job promotion we missed an opportunity to stop and help a hurting colleague?

We believe we are called to something much greater than goals. We are called to sanctification. If you think about it, it is actually quite awesome. We don't have to have it all figured out. We don't have to win the championship to get more worth as a person. We don't have to make more money to be more intrinsically valuable. We can simply love people, serve people, provide value, and do our best to be faithful with what God has put in our hands, and simply TRUST Him.

A compelling mission is much more powerful than a goal. If you are focused on winning a championship, that might empower you for a while; ***but if you are focused on using the transformational power of sports to shape young hearts and minds to become world changers...*** THAT is something we believe will have an exponential impact on the world!

Living With Linguistic Intentionality

Switching from being goal-driven to mission-driven isn't just semantics. When we were young, most of us didn't know the difference between lust and love. The older we get, we start to realize the two are worlds apart.

When we were young, most of us didn't know the difference between happiness and fulfillment. The older we get, the more we start to realize there is an immense difference between the two words.

The difference between being goal-driven and mission-driven is MASSIVE! I think people who are goal-driven have a much greater likelihood of being transactional, and people who are mission-driven have a much greater likelihood of being transformational.

Mother Theresa is a great example of someone who lived a mission driven life. Her mission was to serve the needs of the sick and the dying. You need permission and a license to become a doctor, but you don't need permission to serve the needs of the sick and the dying.

Goals are about achieving, whereas a mission is about who you become.

We encourage "linguistic intentionality." For this very reason, we ask that you not only burn your goals but also wipe the word from your vocabulary altogether. By linguistic intentionality we mean using the most emotionally compelling and beneficial word possible. We think the word "goal" is not the most *beneficial* word we can use. We need a different word and concept altogether, and here's why:

WORDS *put pictures in our mind.*

Pictures in our mind impact how we feel.

How we feel impacts what we do.

What we habitually do impacts our worldly destiny.

If I say "Pink elephant with zebra shoes"

Did you just see that image in your mind?

If you look at a picture of vomit how does that make you feel?

How about a picture of a sunset?

Pictures impact how we feel.

Have you ever said the following, "I don't *FEEL* like doing it"?

How we feel impacts what we do.

What we habitually do impacts our worldly destiny.

It all started with *WORDS*. Words are powerful.

People get paid billions of dollars every year to, add, subtract, and choose specific words for marketing and PR campaigns. Words hold our world together. Think about how the constitution, birth certificates, bill of rights, and laws all hold our world together. When we really think about it, words matter greatly! The Bible says, there is power of life and death in the tongue, and therefore we believe it is imperative we are intentional with every word we use, especially with those we lead.

For these reasons we don't think the word *goal* is the most emotionally compelling or beneficial word we can use. **"Goal talk" tends to shift focus away from the process and place it on outcomes.**

We also have found that goals and outcome-based thinking are so ingrained in our culture that they weigh more heavily in the minds of those we lead. The people we lead have confirmation biases— have a bias towards what *they think* is important.

Here are a few examples of their confirmation biases: WINNING. OUTCOMES. MONEY. POWER.

I have the privilege of working on what I consider to be two of the best coaching staffs in the country, UCLA Women's Basketball, and Oregon Women's Golf.

During a workshop with our team at Oregon, one of the girls said something along the lines of, "we need outcome goals because Coach's livelihood is on the line."

The lady who coaches is mission-driven and does her very best to put the hearts and personal development of those she leads first and foremost. She is by far one of the best at mission driven leadership I've ever seen. YET, this is still how one of the people on her team felt.

She couldn't believe what she heard because she never said anything like that to her team and never would. But here is the thing: we might tell the people on our team about the process ten or fifteen times in a row, but as soon as we mention an outcome it weighs SO MUCH MORE to them.

They internally say, "SEE! I KNEW IT! All that process crap.....the outcome is all that REALLY MATTERS!" It isn't what you are saying, but it is what they are hearing. If this can happen to so heavily driven by mission, then it is probably happening with your team or group.

Everywhere the people on your team turn, society screams that outcomes and winning are what really matters. It is quite literally all they hear and see when they turn on their TV, listen to music, or see what their friends and family value.

Think about this.....

After a basketball game, what is the first question someone who wasn't at the game asks the person who played? "Did you win?"

Quickly followed up by, "How many points did you score?"

After a round of golf? "What did you shoot?"

After a sales call? "Did you get the client?"

Everyone is telling them what is valued. The outcome.

We believe *outcome* comments outweigh *process* comments something like 250 to 1. **So for every 1 outcome comment you need 250 process comments to balance it out.** Which is why people in leadership FEEL like they talk about the process all the time, but rarely is that what those we lead are HEARING or FEELING. They think they know what REALLY matters, and it is the *outcomes*.

What Goals Can Really Do

We had the opportunity to work with a college program that started out with a great record this season. Everyone on the team was committed to a beneficial process that included extra individual training outside of organized practice and attention to detail through supplemental video study. But as the results started to turn, over the course of 7 days the process went south. It seemed as though each loss resulted in five more people giving up on their individual training until the number of people on their team coming early to do deliberate practice leveled off at 1. The very things that needed to be in place to drive the results in a favorable direction were the very things being neglected *because of* the results. We see this repeatedly in teams and individuals. When we focus on the goal and the ever-enlarging gap between our current place and the mark we set out to achieve, we tend to skimp on the process, which is the only thing that will actually close that gap.

You can also have people and teams who give their very best, who do tons of extra work, have great attitudes, and who still fall short of the outcome or "goal." People in coaching tell us all the time these teams feel like failures at the end of the season. When we ask them if they believe these teams failed, they say, "NO!" But because of an arbitrary goal, they feel like a failure, AND most importantly they are being conditioned to believe that working hard, having a great attitude and consistently giving your best are futile. They say, "Why should I put in all this hard work without a prize at the end?!"

We have to face the hard truth that the people we lead might be becoming more entitled, more likely to cheat the process, less resilient, and carrying a victim mentality because of the way we are conditioning them with our outcome-based goal focus.

A Much Higher Standard

Here is what we've found. Consistently giving your very best, every single day, is a much higher standard than arbitrary goals. When you combine that with your commitment list and the other tenants from true mental toughness, we haven't lowered the bar, we have actually raised it incredibly high, BUT we have raised it in a way that is still 100% controllable.

We aren't sacrificing results by being mission-driven, and most of the time we will get more wins and profits will soar as a result of putting first things first and focusing on controllables and true mental toughness. We don't ever have to talk about results or put any energy into the result. Multiple high level programs have burned their goals, put first things first, focused on true mental toughness, and they have achieved some of the best results in program history. Second things were not suppressed, second things increased!

Three weeks after I told my girl who plays golf to burn her goals she blew out the field and won a tournament at twelve under par with the person in second finishing 5 strokes behind her. The next tournament she didn't score as well, but she is starting to understand that you can't control goals. She is learning that you can control your commitments, true mental toughness, and paradoxically by letting go of the results you can actually play better.

We encourage you:

Take off the training wheels.

Focus on true mental toughness.

Focus on commitments and controllables, because you can't control the results anyway.

Love people.

Serve people.

Provide value.

Burn your goals.

Fall in love with the process of becoming great.

Remember, John Wooden won 10 National Championships, including seven in a row. His overall winning percentage was 80%, and he **NEVER** talked about winning. He focused on the process. He started with the basics. He focused on controllables and commitments. It worked out pretty well for him both in terms of results, and more importantly in his relationships with the people on his team long into their lives.

Make sure you are putting first things first in your life. Focus on giving your very very best, treating people really really well, having a great attitude, and unconditional gratitude, *REGARDLESS* of circumstances.

True Mental Toughness is a much higher standard, and much like bicycles with no training wheels, it's not for the faint of heart.

But those who take them off are in for an incredible journey!

How It All Started

You might have seen some of my story in one of our YouTube videos, but I want to give you the whole story.

I played 3 years of college soccer, was suspended from the team 5 times in 2.5 years, and had mediocre statistics at best. Our soccer program was cut after my junior year. I had no schools asking me to come play for them. So, I hung up my cleats and didn't touch a ball for 8 months. Then I went out for the club soccer team at our school, because if I had a scholarship to play on the varsity team, I figured I could play for the club team.....

Then.....they cut me!

3 months later, Joe Germanese, who had transferred to Duke after our program was cut, called me and asked if I was interested in playing at Duke??

What?? Interested, in playing for the #1 team in the country?

"I think the better question is, is the #1 team in the country interested in the guy who had mediocre statistics in 3 years, who was kicked off the team 5 times, AND WHO THE CLUB TEAM JUST CUT 3 months ago, ARE THEY INTERESTED IN ME?!!!"

By the grace of God, I got a full ride scholarship to play on the #1 team in the country from a word of mouth recommendation from the coach who kicked me off the team 5 times.

But then I got to Duke and found myself the last pick on the team during pick up games. It's one thing if those coaching you think you suck, but MY TEAMMATES thought I was the worst at soccer on the entire team.

At that same time I was taking a sport psychology class with Greg Dale and he told us he thought sports were over 70% mental. I thought he was crazy, because if sports were over 70% mental, WHY HAD NO ONE TAUGHT ME TO TRAIN MENTALLY?!!

It seemed if that were true that SOMEONE would have taught me how to train mentally growing up!!!

I thought he was crazy and full of it, BUT I had nothing to lose at that point. I was desperate.

Greg Dale taught us about visualization which I thought was the stupidest thing ever. I laughed when he said, "You can use it to get better at your skills" I was thinking, "THANKS BUDDY, that's why we physically practice! How are we going to know the difference between our visualization and our physical practice?"

But then I came up with a test. I had never scored a goal with my head in my life. In fact, I never really headed the ball in general. So, I decided I would try and use visualization to score a goal with my head. I had no real clue what I was doing, I just tried to see myself scoring a goal with my head, which was complicated by the fact that I hardly headed the ball, so I didn't have a lot of memories from which to draw.

I spent about ten minutes a day for 2 weeks doing my best to visualize myself scoring a goal with my head.

We were playing against Boston College, who went into the NCAA tournament ranked #1 in the country that year, and a ball got crossed into the box and, without thinking, I made a run and headed it into the top corner of the goal!

No joke, if ESPN covered college soccer it would have been on top 10 plays for sure! I had scored hundreds of goals in my life, but this was easily the most beautiful goal of my life.

The next weekend we played the University of Virginia. We were down 1-0 with 47 seconds left in the game. In a last ditch effort, we sent everyone forward to try and score. A ball got played into the box and I jumped into a pile of guys, closed my eyes, the ball hit the top of my head and floated over the goalie's outstretched hands into the back of the net. It was the ugliest goal of my life, but we ended up winning the game in overtime.

Needless to say, from that point forward I was SOLD on visualization and mental training.

I went from being the last pick on the team to being the first ACC player of the week on our team, the Duke *Student Athlete of the Week*, and I finished second in points on our team to Mike Grella who was arguably the best soccer player in the country that year, AND our team had 15 guys who went on to play professionally. If my commitment to mental training produced these types of results, what could your life look like if you applied yourself to the following principles?

SECTION 2

We've spoken briefly on what we believe to be the most fundamental principles:

- Putting first things first
- Burning your goals
- Focusing on controllables
- Focusing on True Mental Toughness

So how do we put this into practice? If it's true that the important things are who we are becoming and the relationships and influence that we have in the world, then everything in life becomes our training ground. Everything becomes an opportunity to learn and grow because everything that has happened in the past and is happening now is preparing us for the present and future. Simply put: **EVERYTHING MATTERS**.

Let me tell you a story about a carpenter from England named John. He had built hundreds of houses for his company over the last fifteen years, and his work was so good that the company became one of the premiere developers in the country. John worked extremely hard putting in overtime nearly every day, and paying special attention to detail on every project.

One day John decided he was going to retire. So he spoke with his boss about it and they decided he would work one last week. His boss called him in the next morning and asked if he would build just one more house for a very special friend of his. Half-heartedly, John agreed and began work on the house.

Though he had built excellent houses in the past, this build was different. Many times in the past John had pushed through days and months where he struggled to find motivation, but he just didn't feel it on this project. Knowing this was his last go around, John showed up each day with less focus than usual. He bought materials and supplies that were second rate. He delegated a lot of tasks without providing supervision. He only worked the hours he was "supposed to," knowing he could build a house up to code on autopilot. He showed up everyday with little joy and without the drive to be better than he was the day before.

Despite the lack of desire and motivation, the house was built on time and was up to code, although not built to the standard he was used to. Walking into the office, beaming ear to ear, John meets with his boss to shake hands and say farewell. After saying thanks, John walks towards the door. His boss calls to him, "John, one last thing." As John turns to face him, his boss hands him a small box with a ribbon around it. John opens the box and pulls out a set of shiny silver keys. His boss says, "The house is yours. You deserve it." He gave him the keys to the house John just built.

Immediately, John's heart sank. If only he knew that he was building his own house, he would have done it all differently. He would have worked with the utmost passion and precision. He would have spent twice the amount of time and would have showed up every day with a clear focus on the job at hand, knowing that he was going to reap what he was sowing.

When we were growing up, especially in school, we failed to realize we were building our own house. We were always looking for the quick fix and the easy way out. We see this same thing happening with many of the people we have the pleasure of working with today. We do our best to share what transformed our life and what we wish we would have known back then.

This next section is a collection of stories, strategies, principles, and tools that have strengthened countless hearts and minds across the world. When they are understood, applied, and trained consistently over the course of time, they will help close the gap between who we are and who we want to be. While it may be simple, it is not easy. But then again, there's a reason why most people don't strive towards their dreams: it's hard. But remember this, we are all building our own houses. Build wisely!

CHAPTER

Life Doesn't Care What We Want

"You don't attract what you want. You attract what you do and what you believe!!" I yelled this to a middle school assembly, but this principle applies to all of us.

It is easy to feel like we "deserve" something or we should get what we "want" out of life; but this is often not the case.

First off, we don't "deserve" anything good. We are already so fortunate for having been born in the land of opportunity that when we complain about not "deserving this" we sound like someone who won the power-ball lottery saying they are unlucky.

Over 1 billion people on earth don't have access to clean drinking water. Even if you live on the streets in the United States your quality of life is still much greater than at least 2 billion people around the world. Over 3 billion people live on less than three dollars per day.

We didn't do **ANYTHING** to deserve access to clean drinking water. There are people whose faces are being eaten alive from not having access to clean drinking water, so let's leave the "I deserve this" or its friend, "I don't deserve this" idea alone. Google "NOMA" and click on images to see what can happen without access to clean drinking water. I support www.charitywater.org where 100% of donations go directly to building wells and providing clean drinking water to those who don't have access to it.

Now moving onto what we say we want out of life. No one sits around and says:

"I want to live off welfare my whole life."

"I want to attract lots of emotional pain and relationship problems."

"I want to be the worst player in the country."

I've yet to hear someone say these things. Usually you hear them say the exact opposite, but we don't attract what we want, we attract what we habitually do and what we believe.

What we do with our 86,400 seconds is going to attract and repel people, experiences, and resources to us.

For a long time I was really frustrated because I didn't think anyone took me seriously, but here's what I've realized: I DIDN'T TAKE MYSELF SERIOUSLY! If I had taken myself seriously I would have used my 24 hours a day differently!

When I started taking myself seriously I changed what I habitually did, and before too long some of the best in the world were calling my phone asking me to coach and mentor them. **I started to attract different people and resources. BUT only AFTER I changed what I habitually did, did what I habitually get start to change....**

The other principle we have to understand is lag time. When we change what we do with our time we aren't going to get immediate results. BUT if we are CONSISTENT and INTENTIONAL in our new habits and training, eventually that lag time will kick in and we will start to see returns on our investment!

Most of us have experienced lag time when driving a car. There are a few seconds between when you slam the pedal to the floor until the car takes off. In life it might be a few months, or maybe even a few years, but the principle ALWAYS holds true.

The second and equally most important part of the principle is that we mainly get out of life what we believe.

Fill in the blank with the first word that pops in your mind:

Life is _____?
People are _____?
Men are _____?
Women are _____?
Jesus is _____?
(My sport) is _____?
School is _____?
Reading is _____?
Work is _____?

The first word that pops in our heads is usually a pretty good indicator of our belief.

If we believe life is hard, we have a vested interest in doing things to make our life harder. Therefore, we will subconsciously or consciously do things that attract more circumstances our beliefs are in line with.

Ever notice that girls who believe guys are jerks tend to attract jerks??

One afternoon a friend and I hung out and we were walking back to my apartment, and I asked her if she had good time. She said she did and that "those girls were REALLY nice."

I got a confused look on my face, and I asked, "aren't most girls really nice?"

She said, "OH NO! MOST girls are really catty." I have told this story in enough workshops with girls nodding their heads saying "exactly" to know my friend isn't the only one who believes girls are catty.

I immediately switched from date mode to teaching mode, and I said, "Whoever most girls are, do you think that in SOME area of their life they aren't catty?" She very hesitantly responded, "I'm sure in SOME area of their life they aren't." I said, "OK, good. So this means they aren't robots, and it also means we play a vital role in the interaction. And if you believe girls are catty, then you have a vested interest in them behaving in that manner, so you will subconsciously or consciously do things to bring that behavior out of them. That way you get the pleasure of saying, "SEE!!! Girls are catty!"

We do this with all of our beliefs, and many times when we form a detrimental belief we do so from a place of emotional pain to try and protect us from future pain. But what usually happens is our belief actually becomes the main impediment to attracting what we want. By believing women are evil, life is hard, people are fake, school is stupid, and reading is boring, we actually guarantee we are going to repel almost anything contrary to our beliefs to keep our model of the world correct. This is a very sad cycle for many people. The pain they experienced has closed them off to the beautiful and amazing in life, and all but guarantees they will attract exactly what they believe.

Dr. Alan Goldberg suggests that, "players [and really all people] are limited most by what they believe is possible." I agree.

I was out training a young boy who plays soccer a few months back and I played a ball to his less dominant foot. As soon as he saw the trajectory of the ball, he let out a cry of "Oh no, not my left foot!"

I smiled and walked towards him, knelt down and asked, "Why don't you want to use your left foot?"

"Cause my left sucks," he said.

"Why do you say it sucks?" I probed.
"Cause I'm not any good with it!" he said dejectedly as he stared at the ground.

"Why aren't you any good with it?"
He shrugged before saying, "Probably because I don't use it."

With a puzzled look on my face, I paused before I said, "So let me get this straight. You believe your left foot sucks. So you don't use it. And because you don't use it much, every time you do use it, it sucks. And then you continue to believe it sucks. And if you continue to believe it sucks, then you don't use it. Is that right?"
"Yeah, I guess," he said puzzled.
"How's that working out for you?"

Now here is the key with beliefs: they are not just thoughts we ascribe to or picture quotes we hang on the walls. The word "believe" in the Greek New Testament of the Bible actually means, "to trust." We've all heard the phrase *you have to walk the walk before you talk the talk* because it's our words **and** actions combined that really show we trust or believe something. And it is our beliefs that underpin what we habitually do.

What are four beliefs that you have about yourself that you think might be holding you back? I never would have verbalized this, but after some introspection and prayer I realized that one of my dominant beliefs was that God would not give me the things I really *really* wanted. Once I verbalized that, I went and objectively looked at the evidence and realized the belief was unfounded. Since then I have consistently, not daily, sown this belief: "I believe that my father created the entire universe and holds the keys to the storehouses in heaven. I know that as I abide in Him and His words abide in me that the desires of my heart will be reshaped and He will give me what I desire." This has caused me to *do* different things and has resulted in a massive change in how I approach the future.

If you want to get different things out of life you MUST change what you believe and this will not happen overnight. But if you are constantly working on changing your beliefs you will get different things out of life. **If you are holding onto detrimental beliefs, even if you are using our 86,400 seconds in the most beneficial ways, it is similar to hitting the gas pedal and break pedal at the same time. It's only going to lead to more frustration, and ironically it will create a belief that what you do doesn't really matter, that you are a victim of circumstance.**

I want to be crystal clear about something here: **I'm not saying your beliefs are right or wrong**. What *YOU* have to ask yourself is this: "Is this the MOST beneficial belief for my life?"

Dr. James Richards says "you might temporarily rise above or sink beneath your heart's beliefs, but eventually equilibrium will set in and we will fall in line with exactly where we believe we are supposed to be." Most people spend their energy focusing on temporary results rather than targeting their heart beliefs. Many of our beliefs were formed when we were very young through emotional events and through influential people in our lives. We influence our beliefs through:

What we **READ, WATCH, and Listen to.**

Who we **SURROUND OURSELVES** with.

What we **VISUALIZE.**

How we **TALK TO OURSELVES.**

What we **HABITUALLY DO.**

Over time your beliefs will shift as you deliberately and consistently subtract detrimental behaviors and beliefs and add more beneficial behaviors and beliefs in your life.

I want to be clear about one more point. You will be uncomfortable doing this in the beginning. Sometimes it will feel like you are being fake.

We call it being *intentional* and disciplining your heart and mind.

Those who play sports at the collegiate or professional level do not want to train everyday for hours on end, but they do it to discipline their bodies so their bodies will perform on command. We can do the same thing by being deliberate and intentional in disciplining our hearts and minds.

When I started being intentional it felt very fake, and that was because the choices I had made in certain situations for most of my life formed super highways of muscle memory in my mind. Those choices had become habitual ways of being. Over time after making new choices, and failing thousands of times, it is now more natural for me to respond with kindness, patience, and love. It didn't happen overnight, but eventually with new choices, new roads were built in my brain.

If you aren't happy with what you are getting out of life, take an open and honest look at what you habitually do and believe. With different consistent choices and changes in beliefs, you too can develop new ways of being, and you just might start getting more of what you want out of life ☺

TRAIN To Be Clutch

- We have a vested interest in creating and attracting what we believe about the world. If I believe people are fake, I will subconsciously or consciously do things to bring out those behaviors from them to justify my beliefs and say "SEE!!! People are fake!"

- It is not whether or not your beliefs are right or wrong. The question you must ask yourself is this: "Is this the most beneficial belief for my life?"
- It will take consistent effort and time to change your beliefs, but it is possible over time.
- We constantly reinforce our beliefs through the fuel we put in our heart:
    - -What we **READ, WATCH, and Listen to.**
    - -Who we **SURROUND OURSELVES** with.
    - -What we **VISUALIZE.**
    - -How we **TALK TO OURSELVES.**
    - -And what we **HABITUALLY DO.**
- Until you change what you do with your 86,400 seconds every day, and until you change your beliefs you will continue to get similar results. Make sure you are seeking out and applying the best strategies from people who are the type of people you want to be like.
- What are four beliefs that you have about yourself that you think might be holding you back? What are four beliefs that you want to adopt that will be more beneficial for your life?

Who Is In Your Circle?

One of the most important decisions we continually make in life is with whom we spend our time. Most people don't spend a lot of time thinking about it, BUT those we spend time with greatly influence how we view the world and what we think about.

It doesn't take a rocket scientist to realize if you think about something for long enough it is going to impact everything in your life. How many times have you seen people talk themselves out of doing something because they can't stop thinking about everything going wrong?

What we spend our time thinking about matters greatly, and who we spend our time with impacts what and how we think.

I read somewhere we tend to be the average of the five people we spend the most time with. So if those five people make an average of 75k per year, you probably make 75k per year. If those 5 people watch an average of 15 hours of TV per week, you probably watch an average of 15 hours of TV per week. We could play this out for books read, vacation days, and many other factors in life.

Who is in your circle—who are you inviting (deliberately or not) to impact and transform your mind, heart, and beliefs?

Eric Thomas, www.etinspires.com, defines 'triple darkness' as "you don't know, that you don't know, that you don't know." So many people are stuck in triple darkness because of their circles. Your circumstances can change, but if you don't change your circle, you might get sucked right back down. Do we need any more evidence than the really sad story of Aaron Hernandez?

When I began my undergrad there was a guy who told me how everything worked in college. He more or less said, "This is how you use your time, who you hang out with, how much you sleep, how you talk to girls, this is how much time you commit to practice, and here's how you study." I bought it, lived it, and paid for it! Guess what year he was. An *INCOMING FRESHMAN!!!* If we are serious about the type of person we want to become and where we want to go, we need to surround ourselves with the wisdom of people who have been there, done that, and have lived to share their mistakes. As Condoleezza Rice encouraged, "Find mentors that don't look like you."

When anything important happens in my life, I call the people in my circle. Before I publish an article, I read it to my circle. Before I have a tough conversation, I talk to the people in my circle. When I am faced with a hard decision, I talk to my circle. The book of Proverbs talks a lot about seeking wise counsel. Many of us seek counsel; it's just not very wise counsel.

In the chapter "Everything Has Hit The Fan" I talk about one of my athletes tearing her ACL and the advice I gave her compared to the advice she was getting from other people. I am in her circle and I influence how she thinks and what she does. I even let her borrow the book, *In a Pit With A Lion On a Snowy Day*. We all need wise counsel, and our circle is where we usually go to get it.

I ask people in workshops all the time, "If you spent 30 minutes a day with me, do you think that would change the way you think?" Most of the time they emphatically shake their head, YES! I tell them that is easily possible because of technology. They can listen to my mp3's, they can read what I've written, and they can watch my videos.

I don't just tell other people to do this, I do it myself. Everyday I listen to Judah Smith for an hour, sometimes more. Judah is very busy, and I might not be able to *physically* have him in my circle, but I am able to have him in my circle nonetheless.

Today, I get to coach and mentor a lot of amazing people, but it wasn't always like this. There was a time 4 years ago when no one was asking me to mentor them, but that was when I changed my circle. Certain people had to go. They were negatively influencing my decisions and it was my responsibility to change how I spent my time and who I spent it with.

The majority of my circle at that time came from spending time with Lincoln, Steve Jobs, Jesus, MLK, and other people who have lived lives I want to model. We may not have physical access to the ideal people for our circle, but we all have access to books, mp3's and videos where we can bring the greats into our circle.

Here is one of Condoleeza Rice's masterclass <u>videos</u> with only 20k views. Here is the <u>video</u> of an hour long interview with, Warren Buffet and Jay Z, done by Steve Forbes, that has 600k views. That might sound like a lot, but to put it into perspective, "*I Love The Way You Lie*" by Eminem and Rihanna has over half a billion with a *B*.

You don't have to be a jerk or tell the people of your current circle that they have been negatively influencing you. You can treat them very well. But make a conscious choice to spend your time differently. If you don't like the influence they have on you, you need to exercise boundaries and choose to spend less time with them. If they are upset because you don't want to do the things they want to do, then that friendship is clearly a transactional one: *affirm what I value and do or else!*

It's never easy to spend less time with people you have been around for a while, but at some point you have to remember that *you* are the one who is building your own house. Your choice creates your challenge. You never know, they might start following you when they see things in your life starting to change for the better. Maybe they will call you names and treat you poorly, but either way, how they treat you is outside of your control.

If you feel stuck, or like you haven't made it to the level you are capable of, take a hard look at who is in your circle. If you are frustrated with the things that keep happening in your life, take a hard look at those with whom you are spending your time. If you are continually finding yourself at the wrong place at the wrong time, take a hard look at your circle. *If you want to achieve your greatest potential, you must surround yourself with people who love you deeply, believe in you, encourage you, BUT who are also willing to challenge you to become the best you are capable of being.*

TRAIN To Be Clutch

- Who are the five people with whom you spend the majority of your free time?
- Which direction are those people pulling you: closer to your dreams or further away from them?
- How many of them are living their dreams or at the very least are passionately chasing their dreams?
- Who are some people who have accomplished a similar dream to yours that you could start learning from? Remember, they don't have to be alive, and you don't necessarily need access to them. You can study them from afar with books and YouTube.

The Day Everything Changed For Me

In February 2009 while living in the closet of a gym my client list totaled three middle school boys. They did not play at the professional, collegiate, or even high school level. They were just young kids who were passionate about basketball and football.

One day I was in the gym all by myself and got really frustrated that I only had three kids to train. I've always been a little optimistically delusional, and I believed despite the fact that I was living in the closet of the gym, I could help any of the world's best in athletics.

I literally yelled out at God, "Why do I only have three kids? I could help Tiger Woods, Lebron James, or Michelle Wie. WHY DO I ONLY HAVE THREE PEOPLE?!"

I felt Him punch me in the chest so strongly with, "UNTIL you value those three little kids the same way you would, Tiger, Lebron, or Michelle, you will NEVER work with a person of that caliber."

Not much has ever hit my heart in such a strong way. My actions and beliefs drastically changed that afternoon in the gym. I did a 180 and have done my best to never look back.

I started treating the kids I GOT to work with as if they were the most valuable and incredible people in the world. I've tried to never forget that and treat all the opportunities and relationships I've been given as if they are that *dream* client or that *dream* friendship.

Two years later I was doing the biggest workshop I had done up to that point. I was supposed to start at 8am the next morning. I was with the guy serving as the head coach all day, so I didn't get to put the final touches on my presentation. All sorts of negative thoughts were going through my head.

"Are you really worth this much money?

You don't belong here.

You are a fraud.

They are going to expose you.

You should just go back home and get a REAL job."

Then to further complicate things I got a text message from one of my interns, "Hey, I really need to talk. Are you free?"

Are you kidding me?! Right now? You want to talk right now? Don't you realize I have a BIG opportunity in front of me, and you are just a little opportunity?

Then it hit me. If NBA all-star Chris Paul had texted me and asked to talk, would I have called him? Of course I would have, and I would have talked to him until 8am if that was what he needed. So, I needed to do the same thing for my intern.

I called her, and never mentioned what was going on in my life, or that she was prolonging my preparations for the next day. I did my best to be fully present, listen, and pour into her as best I could.

I got off the phone and less than two minutes later Jamie called me. At this point Jamie was still playing professional soccer and I was coaching him mentally. Once again, I had those same thoughts go through my head, and then I spent the next hour on the phone serving his needs without telling him about my circumstances.

When I got off the phone with Jamie it was past 1 AM and I still had to put the finishing touches on my presentation. I spent the next hour or so on my presentation, and then finally went to bed. The presentation and my time with the team the next day went really well, and I still work with their program to this day. But more importantly *I stuck to my principles*.

It is so easy to look at what everyone else has: their relationships, their clients, their resources, their opportunities, and say, "Well, if I had that _____ THEN I would do _____." The harder but wiser thing to do is the very best we can with what God has already placed in our hand. If we don't treat our Honda Accord well, we probably aren't going to treat our Mercedes any differently. Now we might for a few months, but eventually, we will treat it the same way we did the Honda Accord.

I call that day in the gym the day everything changed for me because ever since I started valuing and treating every person and opportunity as if it was the opportunity of my dreams, everything has changed in my life.

Today, I get to work with people who have a slightly higher public profile, but if Eric Sheets (my first kid from the gym) texts me, he knows he can get a hold of me just like anyone else I work with. And if he wants to train, I will make the time for him.

TRAIN To Be CLUTCH

- Value what you have as if it was your dream opportunity, client, relationship, friendship, team, coach, etc...

- What opportunities are in your hand that you have been looking past and not valuing?
- Who do you need to treat as if they were your dream client?
- What is something that the three people you are closest to bring to the table? Give them a specific and sincere compliment.
- What could your relationship look like if you consistently treated your significant other as if they were your dream partner?

Hitting Rock Bottom

August 1, 2009 is the date I moved across the country into the homeless shelter to do a volunteer internship in a big city where I had no friends or family for hundreds of miles. When my internship was finished I got a serious upgrade in living conditions and moved into the closet of a gym. During this phase of life I was so broke there were many times my friend and I would be eating turkey out of the package because we couldn't afford anything else.

I grew up relatively poor. My dad grew up in a trailer park. I can vividly remember dreaming about getting a happy meal, but it was my "rich" babysitter that got it for me in my dream. I knew my parents would never spend money on a happy meal. Even my dreams were realistic when I was young!

My dad worked very hard and went from living in a trailer park and selling drugs, to becoming one of the most successful eye surgeons in Oklahoma. As I started puberty our life became much more comfortable financially as my dad became successful. So, I had a decent idea of what it was like to live on both sides of the fence. Most importantly, I knew where you started didn't determine where you finished. I also learned the amount of money in your bank account didn't define you.

Living in the closet of the gym was something that had very little impact on my self-esteem, and I was very straightforward with people about where I lived. My go-to first date was typically a play date at the gym. However, at that time I still felt like some people didn't take me very seriously because of my living conditions. It is funny how life works, because now when people know I was willing to sacrifice and live in the closet of a gym instead of in the comforts of our family home in Tulsa or our condo in Mexico, people are so inspired by my dedication to following my dreams. It's safe to say not many people felt that way when I was actually living in the closet of a gym!

A cool thing happened when I lived in the homeless shelter and the gym closet: I learned I can make it and life still goes on even if you hit rock bottom. Everything is still ok. God still loves me. I can still pursue my dreams, even from the bottom. Some people might say, well that isn't rock bottom, it's not like you were living on Skidrow. Skidrow in downtown Los Angeles, at any given time is home to over 20k people living on the street. It just so happens, at this point in my life, I spent a night sleeping on the streets of Skidrow. I definitely wouldn't want to live there full time, and it definitely shifted my paradigm, but I think it released me from much of my fear.

Many times our fear is much greater than the thing that we fear. When we actually have a small dose of the thing we fear, we often realize it wasn't nearly as bad as we thought. What we thought was a mountain was really only a mound.

When I was 12 years old there was a huge water slide at *Schlitterbahn* Water Park in Texas. It felt like the top of the slide was in the clouds it was so high! I remember the fear increasing exponentially, step by step, as we walked up the steps to the entry point. As I looked out over the entire park my stomach was in such knots I thought I was going to fertilize the ride with my pb&j lunch. It must have been ten minutes of letting other people go in front of me before my dad finally convinced me to get in the little rocket ship looking slide. Tears were pouring down my face as the bottom opened up and I dropped to what I thought would be my young death.

Once I got to the bottom, I had enjoyed it so much I sprinted up the stairs to do it over and over again. My fear had been much greater than the actual experience. Sometimes in life we can be exhilarated and liberated by actually experiencing our greatest fears. That's what happened to Joanne.

Joanne came up with a big idea in 1990, but within six months her mother suddenly passed away. She was living in England at the time, and decided to accept a teaching job in Portugal to try and escape the grief.

Shortly after moving to Portugal she falls in love and gets married. Less then three years after being married her husband abandons her with their three year-old daughter. She moved to Scotland to be closer to her sister. Joanne was living on welfare and had hit rock bottom.

She started writing the story that was birthed back in 1990. Eventually she gets a publishing deal and is given a three thousand dollar writing advance. The publisher didn't think much of the work and only published a limited number of books. They also asked Joanne to create a pseudonym to write under to disguise her identity as a female writer, and hopefully attract male readers. Joanne doesn't have a middle name, but her mother's name was Katherine, so she wrote under the name J.K. Rowling. You are probably familiar with her work. That first book she wrote was Harry Potter, and the Harry Potter series made Joanne the first female billionaire author. Those original copies of Harry Potter have sold for tens of thousands of dollars individually.

"I was set free because my greatest fear had been realized and I still had a daughter that I adored, and I had an old typewriter and a big

idea. And so rock bottom became a solid foundation on which I rebuilt my life."-Joanne Rowling

Having little helps us be more grateful when we have more. Creating when you have few resources makes you resourceful. If you have been molded with the necessity of resourcefulness you learn to do more with less, and you no longer fear rock bottom. You know you can create much from little.

We often fall in love with the idea of being given an abundance of resources and what we would do if we had the resources _____ has. But if we learn to be resourceful with what we have, we will attract so much more. Ever notice banks loan money to those who don't need it?

Rock bottom can be the most liberating and freeing place to operate from. I'm not afraid of losing everything, because I've lived in the closet of a gym, I've slept on concrete, and I've learned how to create much with little. I've been refined through this process and it frees me up to chase my dreams with courage and swiftness.

We can't simultaneously operate out of fear and love. Perfect love casts out fear. Sometimes the realization of our fears is the best thing that can happen to us. Sometimes losing the job we hate is the kick in the pants to actually pursue our dreams. Sometimes losing the championship makes us realize people love us for who we are and not just what we accomplish. Sometimes running out of money forces us to be really creative.

Maybe your fears have been holding you back and it's time to start chasing them instead of letting them chase you. Our greatest pain, our rock bottom, can be the birthplace of our greatest passion and our most inspiring creations.

TRAIN To Be Clutch

- List out 5 things that really terrify you right now? Is there any way you can expose yourself to a small dose of those fears?
- During the next 5 days notice the moments when you say, "I/ we need _____." Is that actually true? Or is there another way to do something using the resources you do have?
- Remember that out of the darkest of days come some of life's greatest moments.

"They" Will Try And Kill You In The Process

We pretty much come out of the womb creating and exploring. Ever notice young kids often get more enjoyment out of the boxes than the toys?

But then we start school and we are told to sit down, shut up, and get in line. And then we wonder why we have an obesity epidemic. We wonder why we lack initiative and creativity.

If you don't do what "they" say, they call you disobedient, unassimilated, disturbed, or worse ADHD. Then they drug you, all to get you to fit in their nice little box.

We are no longer in the industrial revolution and many of the skills kids are learning in school will have to be relearned in order to be successful in the real world. According to Sir Ken Robinson, schools kill creativity.

We weren't created to sit still and learn the "right" answer. We were created to explore, create, love and learn.

If you put one crab in a bucket, it will crawl out. If you put multiple crabs in a bucket, they will pull each other down every time one starts to crawl out. We live in a society of crabs.

They called John Wooden crazy when he tried to run a press for the entire game. They also thought it was crazy he didn't scout opponents; rather, he chose to focus on letting the other team worry about stopping his team.

The board at Apple ran Steve Jobs out of the company calling him crazy and reckless. 12 years later and months away from bankruptcy they came crawling back begging him to come back and save them. He took Apple from the fringes of bankruptcy to one of the most successful and innovative companies of all time.

A massive oak tree comes from a single persistent nut. You have to be crazy to change the status quo. It's not supposed to be easy. You were created to be unique, not to fit into a box. **Be careful who you get advice from. Many people have a vested interest in seeing you fail. If you succeed and show it's possible, then they no longer can say it's "impossible."**

"They" wanted to have the person committed who came up with the idea of television. "They" thought the idea of a 24 hour sports network was stupid and could never work. "They" called Nelson Mandela a terrorist. "They" called Jackie Robinson unthinkable names. Rest assured, "They" will call you all sorts of names, they will throw down the gauntlet in front of you, they will do everything they can to keep you inside their "safe" container.

Be courageous. Once you break out they will call you a genius, and tell everyone how talented you are. They will try and neatly sweep all your years of sweat, turmoil, and uncommon persistence under the rug. It's so much more comfortable to believe talent is reserved for the chosen few than it is to work your ever-loving ass off to become the best you are capable of being.

TRAIN To Be Clutch

- In his book, *How To Stop The Pain*, Dr. James Richards says, "Unforgiveness is like swallowing poison and expecting the other person to die from it."
- Who do you need to forgive so you can move forward?
- Are you spending enough time with people who are living their dreams?
- Are you spending enough time studying the strategies of those who have already accomplished your dream?
- What is a dream you have had for a very long time? You don't have to make it your vocation, but what is the smallest sliver of your dream or passion that you can work on right now?
- You will have many "yes but's" when you are dreaming. Write them down. Many of those have no foundation. Many of those are laughable. Some of those are the very obstacles that provide the way forward. Read *The Obstacle Is The Way.*

Control The Controllables And Leave The HOW To HIM

When people hear that I played soccer overseas they tend to get this romantic idea that I had an agent, shoe deal, thousands of fans, and even a contract.

I didn't.

After my senior year at the University of Memphis, I decided to go to Ireland to try and play. I thought everything was set up for me to have a proper trial period, but when I showed up at the training ground that morning in Dublin, the guy coaching said, "We thought you were joking about coming!"

"Um, well....I'm here, so can I train?" I felt like an idiot!!!

Training was hard. Adjusting to a new culture and new style of play was extremely difficult. And not having any kind of certainty about a direction I was going left me feeling small and insignificant.

For 90 days I bounced around from club to club until finally Shelbourne FC decided to sign me. The contract was less than stellar. I was to be paid two hundred euro a week until they could see me play a bit and raise the wages.

So when I went to file for a work permit to stay in the country I was denied. There was no way that the country, in the financial crisis it was in, would allow me to stay in the country for that little money. Once I was denied, I kept trying to figure out ways to stay.

During my first 90 days I had gotten involved with a small church in Ranelagh and really felt like I wanted to stay and that God wanted me there. So I decided to study at a local bible college while continuing to play ball.

I went in to the immigration office with my application to register as a student. If you have been to an immigration office, then you know how unfriendly those places tend to be. But this time a guy came up to my window and said "Mr. Gilbert, why don't you come to the back with me and we will sort things out."

"Finally!" I thought. "I'm getting the preferential treatment I deserve!"

Well, not exactly. They interrogated me for about two hours in a little white room trying to ascertain my reasons for coming to Ireland in the first place. I didn't know that to get a visa to play ball, that I had to be pursued by the club and invited over.

So, I panicked, and I lied. Or maybe I should say I bent the truth. I honestly did have intentions of trying to enroll in a masters program while there, but found out quickly that I was two weeks too late to enroll. So I told them that I played ball and a guy on the team suggested that I come out and train with his professional team. *That* was the lie.

After two hours, the officers decided that I could stay and study. But there was a condition. The college I wanted to enroll in wasn't a certified institution for foreign students. In order for me to stay in the country and study, they had to get certified in two weeks.

"TWO WEEKS!?! You can't even get money out of an ATM in two weeks in this country!," I thought.

So I began to get all the documents in order that I needed and the college began the process. I tried to control the controllables. But one thing kept nagging at me. I had been dishonest in the meeting with the officials. And it was at that time that I decided to tell the truth moving forward, NO MATTER WHAT!!!!

That sounded like a ridiculous idea to me because I knew the truth was the very thing that would send me home! But I knew that being truthful was part of who I wanted to become and it was honoring God, so it became my focus.

The dominant thought bouncing through my head was, "How God? How will this all work out?"

I didn't use this idea back then, but I have since learned that I have to leave the HOW to HIM. **Do what's controllable, including prayer, and leave the HOW to HIM.**

So I did. For two weeks I heard nothing about progress on the application, but I remained prayerful. I remember thinking about the worst-case scenario. It wasn't that I would go to prison. It wasn't that I would die. The worst-case scenario was that I would return to the sunshine in America, have a car again, work a job that actually wanted me, and eat quality Mexican food. Not too shabby!

Well the day arrived and I wandered to the immigration office and the officer asked me to come outside with him. "Great," I thought, "At least we will be in public and they can't do anything horrific to me!"

I knew that I was going to tell the truth and I knew that the truth was the very thing that could keep me from being where I wanted to be. So I just prayed silently as the officer spoke.

He lit his cigarette and said, "Jamie, your paper work hasn't come through. So I don't know what to do with you."

Suddenly his phone started ringing and he answered it. Prayerfully watching him, I noticed his face start to turn blank. He closed his phone, took another puff of his cigarette, exhaled, and said, "Well that was the office upstairs. They said your college was just approved. I guess you're free to go."

I didn't know what to say. I do however remember being moved to tears as I bolted towards orientation that day.

I didn't have to say anything! And I don't know WHY all of that came through the way it did. But I do know that I did everything in my power to initially keep God from opening that door! It was one of the strongest moments of grace I had experienced in my life.

But one thing I did learn was that I need to control the controllables, and leave the HOW to Him.

I have no idea what kind of doors will open and close in the future. I know that I cannot control results. I have no idea whether or not I will write and mentor in this capacity for the rest of my life. I have crazy dreams about doing things that make no sense! And so I keep coming back to this one principle:

Control the controllables and leave the HOW to HIM.

You Feel That Way
For A Reason

Discipline yourself and others won't need to.
                                        -John Wooden

I learned a valuable lesson on a sunny day in Los Angeles. I was meeting a girl who ran track at the University of Southern California. She told me she loved to run the 100m and the 200m, but she hated the 400m.

Many times I have found we believe our feelings are outside of our control, and they are just there. Sometimes I feel confident and other times I feel like crap. Sometimes I feel good other times horrible.

I asked her to take out a piece of paper and write out the following:

100m and 200m

Focus:

Body Language:

Self-Talk:

400m

Focus:

Body Language:

Self-Talk:

I then asked her to fill it in. During the 100m and 200m what is your focus? What does your body language look like? What does your self-talk sound like? During the 400m what is your focus? What does your body language look like? What does your self-talk sound like?

Her paper ended up looking like this:

100m and 200m

Focus: I *get to* run.

Body Language: Powerful and light.

Self-Talk: I'm going to smoke these girls. I can't wait to run.

400m

Focus: The other competitors, and how fast they are. All things negative.

Body Language: Weak, slower, more lethargic, and heavy.

Self-Talk: Why do I have to run this race? This is stupid. I hate this race.

After looking at this side by side, I asked her if she had a much better understanding of why she might feel a lot more confident and excited about the 100m and 200m races than the 400m races, and she said she did. She was ecstatic to realize there were things 100% inside of her control that were going to greatly impact how she felt about her races.

We all do this. I teach this stuff, and I was at the gym the other day and this is what my chart would have looked like:

Focus: Working out is awful.

Body Language: Lethargic.

Self-Talk: Working out is so stupid. I hate working out. This is so dumb. Let's get out of here already.

Any wonder why I hate working out?? I think not.

During my work with a woman who plays professional golf I decided it would be helpful if we added one other category to the chart.

- Are you operating out of fear, or are you operating out of love?

And here's another one to think about: your facial expression. I know it's hard to evaluate, but think about what your face looks like when you are confident and working hard as opposed to when you are timid or afraid. If you take a second to study LeBron James' face when he catches a ball ready to drive to the rim, it screams confidence and determination. Set up a mirror or get out your camera phone and have a glimpse of what your face looks like when you are feeling strong and confident. Along with the others, wear your face of confidence even when you don't *feel* confident.

The next time you don't feel like doing something, fill out the chart and see if it doesn't hold true. You may not have control over how you feel, but you do have control over what you focus on, your body language, how you talk to yourself, your facial expression, and whether you are operating out of fear or love. Taking action over those might just change how you feel!

TRAIN To Be Clutch

- What is something you absolutely love to do?
  - o What is your focus when you are doing it?
  - o What is your body language when you are doing it?
  - o What is your self-talk when you are doing it?
  - o What does your facial-expression look like?
  - o Are you operating out of fear or love while doing it?
- Now, what is something you hate to do?
  - o What is your focus when you are doing it?
  - o What is your body language when you are doing it?
  - o What is your self-talk when you are doing it?
  - o What does your facial-expression look like?
  - o Are you operating out of fear or love while doing it?
- Do this same exercise for something you are very confident while doing, and something you aren't very confident while doing.
- The next time you don't "feel" confident, try this test.
- The next time you don't "feel" like doing something, try this test.

Raising The Bar

I tweeted this advice to people coaching and playing:

People in coaching: Love and encourage those you lead

People playing: Trust your leaders and give your very best

Both: Fall in love with the journey

I was a little shocked at the firestorm of retweets and favorites this simple tweet set off around the country. So I thought it might be helpful to unpack and elaborate on the idea just a bit.

People in leadership, and this includes parents and those who teach for a living, we need to raise the bar when it comes to loving and encouraging the people on our team and organization. I've seen it countless times, when we make people feel loved, safe, and secure, they will be teachable and run through walls for us.

Please don't misunderstand me when I say we need more love and encouragement. This has nothing to do with lowering standards or being soft. In fact, I actually think it means raising standards. Two of the greatest leaders in history, John Wooden and Jesus, raised the bar for their followers in my opinion. However, I believe they did so with love and grace.

Regardless, or your personal beliefs on Jesus, from a historical perspective, I think we all would agree that his life split time as we know it, as in, B.C. and A.D. So, I think it's worth examining how he led.

Jesus encountered a woman who had been caught in the act of adultery, and after he revealed the hypocrisy of her accusers, he told her he wouldn't condemn her, but then he said, "Go and sin no more." This woman, according to ancient Jewish law, should have been punished by death. However, Jesus showed her lavish grace coupled with raising the bar. It was an incredible balance of love and elevating the personal standards for her life. I don't think Jesus actually believed she would never sin again in her life; but I do believe he had dramatically increased the expectations for this woman.

In Wooden, we find a similar approach. When Bill Walton, who was one of the greatest people to play college basketball, showed up with facial hair to get on the bus for a game, Wooden didn't yell at him and tell him how disappointed he was in his leadership. No facial hair was a clear expectation he always expressed to his teams, and here was the best guy on his team not following the rules. Wooden, told him the facial hair looked good, but that he wouldn't be able to join the team on the bus to the game with it. The bus left without him, and he had to make it to the game on his own if he wanted to play, AND he would have to be clean-shaven.

There was no big scene that was made. There were no exceptions that were made because he was the best in the world at his craft. The team bus didn't stop at a store to get him a razor and shaving cream on the way to the game. He simply told him it looked good, but that he couldn't play on the team with it. I think this is an incredible example of love and raising the standards we all can learn from. It is challenging to respond to the people on our team in love when they fail to meet our expectations, but as exhibited by both Wooden and Jesus, we can simultaneously love them without lowering our expectations for them.

In the summer of 2013 I had the privilege of spending a few hours with Adam Krikorian. I didn't know it when we first met, but he had just won an Olympic gold medal coaching the United States women's water polo team. Later on in the evening I asked him what the most important lesson he learned from the experience, and he told me it was the importance of trust. At the time I wasn't blown away by the answer. But over the next six months I started to realize how fundamental trust is to everything in leadership, and how few leaders actually have it with those they lead.

If people in leadership intentionally cultivate trust with the people on their team, then those people will have an easier time investing in higher standards of living. I've started to see how often there is a trust breakdown, and the people coaching and playing simply don't trust each other. This is a recipe for disaster. If the people playing trust the people coaching them, it is far easier to focus 100% of their energy on controllables, and trust the people coaching them are doing things ultimately in their best interest, no matter how strange or difficult they may be in the process.

So, people in leadership, the question you need to ask yourself is this: Am I trustworthy?

Am I consistent?

If you aren't consistent, it is hard to trust you.

Remember, John Wooden said the softest pillow is a clear conscience. If you aren't sure, then do an anonymous survey asking your team, or ask the captains whether the team trusts you. If they don't, figure out what you have done and be humble enough to work to win back their trust. Maybe it's not your fault, but you can still take responsibility. More and more kids are coming from backgrounds where they have little reason to trust the adults in their lives, so you might be dealing with baggage that you didn't create. However, if you want to maximize your influence and really equip your team for life, you MUST develop deeper levels of trust with the people on your team.

The last thing I touched on in the tweet was: *fall in love with the journey*. No one on their deathbed is going to look back and wish they won more games. They are going to wish they expressed their love to and encouraged more people. Sometimes I tell the people I get to work with that I love them. Sometimes this feels awkward to me, and I know it could potentially get me in trouble. But I learned as a nine year old that life is short. One day I had the most amazing little brother in the world, and the next day I didn't. **Life is short, and tomorrow isn't promised. I might not make it to the next practice or game, and if I don't, I want the people I love to know exactly how amazing I think they are and that I love them.**

How Much Are You Willing To Suffer?

You can ONLY reach your fullest potential by choosing the toughest challenges over and over in life.

How much are you willing to suffer? I mean really suffer.

Because of television all we see is the glitz and glam of the lives of very successful people. But we don't see the behind the scenes and the tens of thousands of hours of training, hustling, and grinding they have been doing.

We don't see them getting up before the sun comes up and working long after it goes down. We don't see all the sacrifice and dedication. We didn't see them working when almost no one believed in them.

Friday night after Friday night, Kevin was in the gym working on his game. One night the janitor came up to him and said, "Kevin why don't you ever go out and party with your friends?" Kevin said, "Parties won't take me where I want to go."

You have to be willing to work when others party. You have to be willing to suffer when others play. You have to be willing to do what others won't, so you can do what others can't. It doesn't happen by accident.

Kevin Johnson went on to receive NBA all star accolades.

Everyone has BIG DREAMS, but the best indicator of whether or not you will have a shot, not a guarantee, but a shot at making your dreams come true is the truth about how much you are willing to suffer.

People are often in awe when they hear about the missions Navy Seals are able to pull off, but for years in training they have CHOSEN to undergo egregious and excessive amounts of suffering. *For example, during Hell Week, they are only guaranteed 4 hours of sleep during 5 days of excruciatingly difficult physically and mentally demanding work.* Their training is the toughest in the world, but through that pain and suffering some of the greatest warriors in the world are created.

Lil Wayne is a rapper on more songs than any other artist, but most people don't know he started writing raps at age 8 and as an 11 year-old he was writing raps for up to 8 hours a day. How many 11 year-olds with little parental guidance, or support, would be willing to "suffer" through that?

We see Kevin Durant's jumper that is wetter than Niagara Falls, and people say he is so talented. But we don't see Kevin Durant in the gym soaked in sweat, intentionally "suffering" 3 hours before practice starts.

Anyone can dream a dream, but the real question is how much are you willing to suffer. How many times will you be willing to say NO to instant gratification in order to say YES to your dreams that are so far off they feel like fairytales? How many times will you seek out the toughest people in coaching who won't just tell you what you want to hear? How many times will you be willing to PERSEVERE in the face of adversity? How many times will you get back up when you get knocked down? How many times will you show up with enthusiasm even though your boss doesn't appreciate your hard work and sacrifice? How many times will you be willing to be called crazy and delusional in the pursuit of your dream?

Remember:

First they will ignore you.
Then they will tell you you are crazy.
Then they will tell you are stupid.
Then they will try to sabatoge you.
And then finally they will try and borrow your money ☺

If you want to achieve your fullest potential and tap into areas of strength, persistence, and courage you never knew existed, continue to take on the toughest challenges and know that your willingness to suffer through the toughest stuff is the greatest predictor of your future success.

TRAIN To Be Clutch

- If you are thinking about the next level, then you need to realize that there is another level you can operate at right where you are.
- Who can you ask about better strategies for training? Where can you find information about the training many of the best in the world do? Hint: books, youtube, and asking good questions!
- What is the next step that scares you? What could you do that would put you outside of your comfort zone? Maybe that's where you should start.
- On the other side of your greatest fears lie some of life's greatest opportunities.
- Read *In A Pit With A Lion On A Snowy Day* by Mark Batterson

Stop Comparing And Focus On Competing

"Who here wants a shot?" I asked holding a tennis ball while standing next to a trashcan during a workshop. All of a sudden the eyes widened, breathing got shallow, people leaned back in their seats, and they began to steal glances at each other as if to say "Please someone else raise your hand!"

The tension rose as the seconds felt like hours. "Okay," I said, "I'll choose someone myself." The anxiety was intense! I tossed the ball in the air to a person in the front row, and as the ball was caught a collective sigh of relief was let out by the rest of the team: as "Thank God it's not me!" was written all over their faces.

Does it surprise you that this was actually a college basketball team?

It's a simple task: toss the tennis ball into the trashcan from eight feet away in front of fifteen teammates. It's not a matter of life and death and it doesn't have any affect on playing time. Each of these people had spent thousands of hours throwing balls into cylinders in much more intense situations!

I asked the young lady who shot and missed what happened. She said, "I was afraid to miss." "Is that really what you were afraid of?" I probed. "No," she said. "I was afraid of what everyone would think about me."

A lot of times in many contexts in life much of our inability to scratch our potential or play hard is down to the fact that we are comparing rather than competing. Competition is great between people on the same team. Someone beats you and you try harder to improve to play better next time. The Bible talks about this as iron sharpening iron.

Comparison is different. Comparison is about worth. He beat me so he is a better person. She trains with the national team so she is always going to get the starting spot. He has closed more deals for the company this year so why should I even bother to try harder? Comparison usually leads to diminished or inflated worth and takes our focus and energy away from things we can control.

Comparison = Better Than
Competing = Getting Better

I once thought I was somebody because I beat a friend in a push-up competition in sixth grade. I also thought I was nobody because I was beaten in a three mile run around a cow pasture in Oklahoma when I was fifteen. You may laugh at these examples, but how many of us actually do the very same things now?

An interesting thing happened this year as I was having individual meetings with people on a college team. I had the opportunity to meet with one of the guys I had never talked to individually. I was excited because he was the one guy who I noticed who exemplified our definition of true mental toughness. He always had a great attitude, he seemed to work as hard as he could both in practice and in games, he treated everyone on the team extremely well, and he was the one guy who consistently competed at a very high level throughout the year. The people coaching loved him and even said that they didn't feel like they needed to say anything to him because he just brought it everyday.

As I was trying to help him articulate a mission for his life, I asked the question, "Do you want to play professionally?" Without hesitation and with a little laughter he said, "No, not at all." Seriously? I mean out of 22 meetings, 21 guys said they wanted to play professionally, at least if the opportunity presented itself. But here was the one guy on the team who I thought because of his process and commitment could actually play at that level, yet that wasn't his goal. **In fact, he shared with me that he had no goals.** What he had was an internal drive to get better everyday, a desire to be an influential part of the team, and a love for competing.

Competition is awesome! **As long as it is competition that *refines* you, not competition that *defines* you.** Moreover, when we talk about competition, we are talking about focusing on getting better, not being *better than* someone else. In Wooden's words, "Don't worry about being better than somebody else, but never cease trying to be the best you can be. You have control of that, not the other." As we let go of comparing our stats with our teammates, stop measuring our performance with that of rival businesses, and stop gauging our worth by the accolades we achieve, we let go of one of the greatest causes of emotional pain and we can thrive by focusing solely on *our* development.

TRAIN To Be Clutch

- We need to remember that the measure we use to judge others is the same measure we use to judge ourselves.
- If we want to begin worrying less about what other people think of us, we need to practice judging less and loving more.
- Your value comes from who you are, not what you do.

- In what areas of your life would you, and others around you, benefit from making the shift from comparing to competing?
- How can you use the abilities and processes of others as a rubric or pacesetter for becoming who you want to become?

Don't Just Go Through It, Grow Through It

The sun had yet to come up and we were walking to the weight room, otherwise known as the "punishment chamber." Most of our freshman class skipped an obligatory school function two days earlier and were now facing 6 AM punishment with Mark Davis. Davis is one of those guys who wears a permanent scowl, rocks a crew cut and doesn't own a shirt with sleeves. His *regular* workouts were some of the toughest around. Seeing someone throw up while lifting weights was a regular occurrence in our weight room. So you could imagine our angst as we faced one of his punishment sessions!

After 45 minutes of pain, Davis tells us to stay out of trouble, and he looks at Joshua and says, "Medcalf, you better give your best next time, today wasn't good enough." Now, Joshua had a knack for saying stupid things and had already been suspended from the team twice that year. Knowing his comment could result in more team punishment, my heart sank.

"I'll be here at 6 AM tomorrow because anything you do to me is only going to make me stronger!" Davis' face turned fire hydrant red and I thought he was going to kill not only Joshua, but everyone in our general vicinity! I feared for our lives.

I didn't appreciate it at the time, but he actually spouted off some deep wisdom.

> *Anything that happens to me today is in my best interest. It's an opportunity to learn and grow.*

What would your life look like if this became your default mode of operation when…
You are stuck in traffic and late to a meeting.
You shank a golf shot.
You are hit with an injury.
You lose a potential client.
You are faced with a significant pay-cut.
You are placed on the bench.
You lose your job.

One of the first questions that probably comes to your mind is, "How or why is this in my best interest?" Here's the deal. You don't need to try and figure out *how* it is in your best interest because we never really understand why things happen. **All we are asking is that you *believe* it is in your best interest so that you direct your energy and focus in the most beneficial and constructive ways possible.**

During one of our workshops a woman who plays golf said to us, "so when I duck-hook my drive into the hazard on number 17 I'm supposed to just believe that it's in my best interest?" Joshua responded, "Yes, what is the alternative? If you are angry about it and dwell on the situation you're likely to not think clearly and hack at your next shot. How's that strategy been working out for you?" Her shoulders dropped a little bit and she confessed it hadn't been working very well.

Again, you don't have to know how or why, you just have to *believe* it is in your best interest.

But here's the kicker: beliefs are not just quotes we say to ourselves. The word "believe" in the Greek New Testament means "to trust." It's words coupled with action. When we were younger my brother built a bungee swing out of old bicycle tubes hanging from our tree. When he said "I believe it's safe. Jamie why don't you try it," I should have responded, "***show me*** you truly believe by going first." But I didn't and I paid for it! Our belief that any situation is in our best interest needs to be coupled with **controllable action**. Let me give you an example.

Joshua was visiting my family in Denver last Thanksgiving and while I was driving him to the airport he realized he hadn't checked in yet. And those of us who choose to fly *Southwest* know that you do not want to check in right before your flight! After he checks in on his phone, rather than a boarding pass with his boarding group and number, his phone tells him to speak with a desk attendant. While I'm laughing he grins and says, "I'm believing it's in my best interest."

Now how would most of us feel if we knew we were the last to check in on a full Southwest flight? We all know that we are going to get the least favorable seat and for most of us, the circumstance will dictate how we carry ourselves. Many of us would have our heads down, we wouldn't be talkative, we'd tear ourselves apart verbally, we'd replay all the bad beats we've gotten in life, and probably have a total disregard for others and serious distaste for finding opportunities.

But as Joshua believed it was in his best interest, his actions began to change. He chose to direct his energy and focus in the most beneficial manner possible. He walked upright, smiled, used the attendants name as they interacted, and was ready for opportunities. While on the tram to the terminal he noticed a cute woman who happened to have a ticket on the same flight. They began talking and she saved him a seat on the plane. Not only did he get a favorable seat, but he met someone whose heart and story has inspired many people across the country. It's funny what can happen when we believe everything is in our best interest.

Now we do not want people to be confused. **Believing that things are in our best interest does not mean the pain, hurt, or struggle are taken out of the situation.** When I woke up to my wife having an early miscarriage in the middle of the night it was not a time to ask *why* questions. For the next 48 hours my focus and energy needed to be directed towards immediate action, comforting Amy before and after her operation, and efficiently relaying the message to our family overseas. If I had focused on why or how, I would have only made the situation worse. I would have wasted energy on things outside of my control, and been a much less helpful husband. There was a time for grieving, but that was not the moment.

Was it painful? Yes. Was it a struggle to be excellent? Yes. But by directing my focus and energy in the most constructive and beneficial manner possible, the situation was made better for everyone.

So, if you duck-hook one into the hazard, you can ask yourself what you would have done differently because there is another shot coming.

If you're out with an injury, great! You have the opportunity to study your team, develop your sport IQ, develop your character, and work on mental training.

If you are benched for a game you can increase your IQ by studying, not just watching the games, and work on being a great encourager.

If you have a fitness session coming up then you have the opportunity to push until failure while working on your self-talk.

If you're stuck in a plane on the runway you can read a good book and learn from the greats.

If your company has failed then you have an opportunity to reflect on how you will do things differently in your next venture.

If your boss takes away the resources you have habitually used to do your job, you can decide that this is a great opportunity to exercise resourcefulness and possibly develop a more efficient way to do things.

Believe that anything that happens to you today is in your best interest, because it is an opportunity to learn and grow.

We are surrounded by opportunities to take drastic strides towards becoming the person we want to be, but we have to have the most beneficial mindset to make the most of those diamonds in the rough. Whatever happens today, don't just *go through it*, **grow through it!**

TRAIN To Be Clutch

- Recall a situation or experience where you believe the more beneficial thing to do would have been to believe it's in your best interest.
  - o   How would you have carried yourself?
  - o   How would you have talked to yourself?
  - o   How would you have treated other people?
- Identify a situation or context you regularly find yourself in that causes anxiety, anger, or stress. What would be the most beneficial way of carrying yourself in that context today?
- Write this statement 5 times: "Anything that happens to me today is in my best interest. It is an opportunity to learn and grow."
- What could your life look life if this was your predominant belief over the next year?
- Take three minutes to watch the <u>Diamonds In The Rough</u> video on the train2bclutch *YouTube* channel.

Stop Thinking Outside Of The Box

Stop thinking outside of the box.

Start habitually acting and experimenting outside the box.

Treat people like people.

Move to another city.

Sell all your stuff.

Move to a foreign country.

Quit your job.

Become a consummate experimenter.

Chase the stuff that scares you.

Most of the things I did scared the life out of me before I did them!

Speak in front of thousands of people? *But I was super shy and introverted growing up!*

Move to one of the biggest cities in the world?! *I don't know anyone there!*

Move into a homeless shelter? *Skipping scholarships to law school will be a huge regret!*

Move into the closet of a gym? *That just sounds crazy.*

Create the first mental training apps in the world for basketball, soccer, and golf? *You have no money and no technology background.*

Share mental training tools and ideas with people at the top of their craft? *You don't even have a psychology degree.*

Write a book? *Who will read it? You don't have a publisher.*

On the other side of the fear people tell you how amazing it is and how inspiring you are, but in the midst of the journey you feel like you are pooping your pants in public wearing nothing but whitey-tighties!!

But the thing is it's not about thinking. Everyone has great ideas. Most people aren't willing to habitually, and consistently act, fail, learn, and repeat outside the box.

It's not an accident and it's not luck. It is habitual and deliberate passion, persistence, and patience in ACTING outside the box.

They will call you crazy and delusional when you start, then they will call you talented and lucky when you get to do the things they can't do because you were willing to do what they wouldn't.

TRAIN To Be Clutch

- In what ways can you begin to experiment right where you are?
- What kind of fear is holding you back from sticking out?
- Who do you know who operates outside the box? Study them!

It Has To Be YOUR Vision Of Success

He was miserable. The people who served with him were miserable. And everyone who listened to him speak weekly was miserable too!

So the leadership team sat him down.

"John, it doesn't seem like it's working out. How do you feel about things though?"

"I don't get it. I went to school for four years to take the role of lead pastor. I wanted to serve in this position for the last ten years of my life! But every time I get up there to speak I feel empty inside. It's like I'm doing something wrong!"

"Well John, tell me this: When do you fell like you really come alive and thrive?"

"I know this sounds terrible, but I *love* it when people die!"

"What!?!"

"NO! I don't love *that* people die! But I really feel like I am operating in my passion when I am serving families that are going through bereavement. When I get to sit and listen to families talk about the best of their loved one who passed I always feel focused. And sharing those stories and God's comfort at funerals really feels fulfilling."

"Well, John, how about you shift your focus towards bereavement and we find someone who feels the same way about teaching each week?"

"Deal!"

This is a true story. Sadly, it's a story that I hear over and over again. There are so many of us that are currently not operating in our dream position. Still some of us have what we *thought* was our dream position, but we feel extremely unfulfilled.

There is a difference between form and function. Most of us get so fixated on the form: starting spot on a particular team, C-level position in a fortune 500 company, head coaching position at a prestigious college, or valedictorian of our class. A lot of us talk about *where* we want to be, but we are not focused on *what* we want to do.

The function, or *what* we want to do, is what I call passion. John's passion was engaging with God's word and engaging with people. But because he had been told success was being in the lead pastor role, he thought getting that position was the goal!

I hear so many people tell me that they want to be in a head-coaching role. When we get down to it, they love sports and love people. They can combine those two in many different ways. It could be at the youth level, through a non-profit overseas, mentoring kids in their local neighborhood, or being a skills trainer at any level. Getting to work with plenty of people in high level coaching, I have come to find that most of those positions require at least 70% of work that is outside actual engagement with sport!

What I am interested in is helping people find their function. Helping them verbalize what really makes them come alive! And you know what, some of the time that means they should probably quit their current job!

So what is your vision of success? Is that *your* definition of success, or is that just what is deemed successful in society?

For too long I thought that to be successful in soccer I had to play at the very highest level. That's what all the people who coached me in youth, high school, and college soccer praised! That's what everyone on television always talked about!

Little did I know that soccer was really a training ground and vehicle that would eventually take me to one of the most fulfilling roles in my life: coaching u-10 girls basketball in Ireland!

What is *your* passion? What is *your* vision of success?

As you discover your passion, the forms will take shape.

TRAIN To Be Clutch

- What makes you extremely mad, overwhelmingly glad, or heartbrokenly sad? Somewhere in there lies your passion.
- You don't need to operate in your passion as a vocation.
- The people who are mission-driven and passionate about their work do things with more creativity, more effort, and outlast those who work for an outcome.
- How can you operate in your passion right where you are? I know a guy who loves to engage with people and find solutions. Everyday he focuses on those two aspects as he manages a car dealership. It's not about selling cars. It's about finding the best vehicle to help that family efficiently live out their dreams.

Is There Something BETTER Than Positive?

Do you remember when you were a kid and you would compete in potato sack races? When you are in a potato sack race you and your partner are extremely dependent upon each other. If you aren't on the same page, you are going to have multiple servings of humble pie, and probably quite a few bumps and bruises from all your falls.

I'd love for you to imagine yourself back in a potato sack with another person, but let's change the setting a little bit. You are in this potato sack and you are on a highway with a semi-truck coming at you 70 mph. Do you want to be in a potato sack with a positive thinker, or a constructive and beneficial thinker?

You can think as positively as you want:

"It won't hurt that bad,"
"I'm sure the semi will be able to swerve around us,"

But I'm "positive" if you don't actually get out of the way, you are going to get squashed like a bug.

Personally? It's not even a question! I'm going with the constructive and beneficial thinker 100 out of 100 times!

The funny thing about the word positive is that positive people already get it and are generally pretty positive. However, the trouble comes with those of us who might bend a little more to the cynical, negative, pessimistic, or whatever word you would like to insert. We, and I definitely include myself in this group, WE have a hard time when we hear this word. Sometimes when I hear, "we just need to be more positive" it kind of makes me want to throw up.

I've even asked people in high level coaching, "when someone tells you that you need to be more positive, do you kind of want to punch them in the face?" And they usually say, "YES!"

So, we believe there is something better than positive.

We are all for more beneficial.
We are all for more constructive.
We are all for more loving.
We are all for more encouraging.

Some would say, that's just semantics, positive means all those things! For some that is exactly how they would define the word positive. BUT, there are some who, when they hear the word positive, they hear fluff, lower standards, and just telling people what they want to hear.

For people in leadership (and we would argue that is everyone), it is especially important for us to have linguistic intentionality in our words. Our words are powerful and there is something deeper and more beneficial than positive.

So, rather than positive self-talk, we should have constructive and beneficial self-talk. You are not lowering standards and feeling like you are letting yourself off the hook for mistakes and subpar play; rather you are simply using constructive and beneficial self-talk that directs your focus and energy in the most helpful manner possible.

Rather than positive body language, we should have powerful body language, or coachable body language. And while we are on the topic of body language, the people coaching tend to be quick to point out when the people on their team have poor body language. But you need to take a hard look at the game tape for what kind of body language *you* model everyday in practice and at games. Most of us stomp our feet, throw our arms, roll our eyes, and throw temper tantrums when the people on our team miss layups, fail to grasp a concept quick enough, or make some other mistake. Powerful body language is something we ALL can get better at!

TRAIN To Be Clutch

- What are some words you can use instead of positive?
- What are you actually trying to say when you use the word positive? Do you mean encouraging? Do you mean powerful? Do you mean loving? Do you mean going in a beneficial direction?
- One exercise that could serve useful is to write out some of the "Do Not Use" words and phrases on a notecard, and then beside it write "Use This Instead" and write out some phrases that are more beneficial.

Dig In Or Drift On

A mentor of mine once told me a story. He grew up on the west coast by the beach where he and his friends used to play almost daily. One of the games they used to play taught me a great lesson.

He said they used to go out in the water right where the waves were breaking. The object of the game was to try and stand in one place as long as possible while the waves were beating against you.

They would do this day after day, week after week, until he finally figured out the key to standing firm. You see, most of the guys would get pummeled by a wave and their feet would shuffle under water and when the waves were being pulled back out into the ocean they would move their feet into a new position again before the next wave came.

But my mentor started to realize that this strategy wasn't working. So he decided that after being hit by a wave, he was going to try as hard as he could to dig his feet down into the sand. Instead of shuffling his feet while the water went back out to sea, he wiggled his feet deeper and deeper. It wasn't easy and no one else was doing it, but that's why he figured it might work.

In his mind, he only needed to withstand the first three or four waves until he would have a secure base.

The waves crashed against him, he stubbornly withstood the resistance and the urge to try a new spot, and dug his feet a little deeper each time.

After a few minutes, he realized that all of his friends had moved about fifty yards down the beach being pulled by the undertow and current.

Meanwhile he was fighting, digging in, and eventually the sand was up to about the middle of his calves so that he was able to withstand the waves crashing.

Strength is only built through resistance. But too often we avoid the resistance at all costs. Some of us don't want that feeling of desperately gasping for air so we don't do fitness drills that bring us to failure. Some of us don't want to look foolish in front of our boss and therefore we choose to only do what is asked of us instead of tinkering with creative solutions.

Many of us, however, choose to take on resistance, but when it becomes consistently difficult, we shuffle. We try a new workout, buy new equipment, get a new person to coach us, fire our current staff, or move to another team or business. **But it's the willingness to stand firm in one place, one strategy, and to a small set of principles that allows us to develop the characteristics needed to thrive in any situation.** Sometimes I think those of us who have a stubbornness about us are better off. If we can direct that stubbornness towards being ruthlessly boring to our process, many times its that unwillingness to change that can take us to new heights. Joshua has said this from day one: **Even a poor strategy will succeed with passion, patience, and persistence.**

Some of us stand firm by digging in. Others of us drift along by shuffling our feet.

Train To Be Clutch

- What are some areas in your life where you think relentless stubbornness to a single process would benefit you?
- What are some of the waves that you will have to endure in the process?
- What are some of the things that you will choose to say NO to that will allow you to stand firm?

This Is So Simple I Bet You Won't Even Apply It

I felt WAY in over my head.

Sitting on the front row was a guy with a documentary on Netflix about his life. Next to him was a guy who had one of the most recognizable names for the last twenty years in the league. Somewhere in the back was a guy who was a national hero, and who played in three world cups as well as the English Premiere League.

During the workshop I hadn't seen a group of people that disinterested in what I had to say since I tried to give a talk in the housing projects of south central Los Angeles.

I cut the workshop an hour short, because I could tell everyone wanted out.

I then quickly apologized to the person in charge for failing.

He looked quite puzzled, and then he told me quite a few of the guys had said they really enjoyed it.

I was perplexed as I went back to my room, but his comments made me feel a bit better as I prepared for my individual meetings with the guys on the team.

From reviewing their intake forms I quickly realized all of their biggest challenges were things happening outside of their control: get a better contract, earn a starting spot, make the team.

So, after I asked the first guy about his biggest challenges I told him I had a great strategy for him.

He leaned it and was obviously ready for it.

I told him, I want you to have a great attitude, I want you to give your very very best, and I want you to treat people really really well!

He, and every other guy I met with had the exact same body posture response: They all leaned back, crossed their arms, and completely disengaged.

I knew what I asked next was my last hope to get through to them, so I asked each of them a simple question: **"Can you name one person on your team who does those three simple things EVERY single day?"**

Not one of them was able to.

I said, "So, here is what I want you to do. Focus on having a great attitude, giving your very very best, and treating people really really well, EVERY single day."

In my experiences we sometimes forget simple doesn't mean easy. We also forget that if it is easy to do, it is also easy *not* to do.

The New England Journal of medicine shared an interesting study about how a new procedure saved 1,500 lives, reduced infection by 66%, and saved over $75,000,000, all in less than two years from implementing this new procedure.

Do you know what the procedure was?

A simple checklist.

Everyone knew to do the five things and they were very basic, for example, one of the items on the checklist was the Dr. was to wash their hands. But it's crazy how easily we overlook the small, crucial, and fundamental processes in our disciplines.

It's amazing the results you can get when you never skip steps and you do the simple things very well.

TRAIN To Be Clutch

- What are some of the fundamentals in your discipline? Examples might be:
  o Golf: setup, grip, balance, ball placement, takeaway, finish, etc.
  o Leadership: Specific and sincere compliments, read, ask good questions, beneficial body language, etc.
  o Basketball: communicate loudly, athletic stance, active hands on defense, box out, keep cutting, etc.
  o Business: read, make calls, communicate clearly, ask good questions of colleagues, listen before speaking, etc.

October Is Coming

I had a full calendar for the summer. I had the opportunity to work some top class people who were excelling in their industry, we had a new style of workshop that we were beginning to do, and for the first time I was working with a group in the public sector.

There was way more than enough in there to put me outside of my comfort zone and the more that I glanced at the calendar, the more anxiety I felt wondering how everything would pan out.

As soon as I became aware of my wandering mind and limiting beliefs, I said these words to myself: "Jamie, October is coming."

I remember hearing a story about a guy who was pitching in the major leagues who seemingly had ice in his veins during the World Series. When someone asked him how he was so cool under pressure, he said that he knew a week from now, barring any catastrophic event, he was probably going to be back at his home in the Rockies with his family. All of the craziness would pass. A new season would approach. And he would likely be reflecting on how small that event seemed in the rear view.

Have you ever been there? You get to the other side of a crazy week, huge event, massive meeting, or tournament and turn around laughing at how ridiculous the anxiety was that you had!!!

For people in sport I always ask them how important their middle school tournament was three years later. It never carried that importance they thought it would!!!

"October is coming," reminds me that in a few months I am likely to be on the other side of some of the bigger challenges that I see in front of me right now. Regardless of how those events turn out, I am very unlikely to be without a home, water, or my family as a result. But in a few months I know I am going to look back on how I carried myself during that time and I want to be proud of the way I moved forward and tackled those fears.

"October is coming" also reminds that in a few months I am likely to have more big challenges ahead of me that make the current challenges very small. And if I am not intentional I will face the same anxious thoughts over and over as challenges face me throughout life.

"October is coming" also reminds me that there is no such thing as a big break. I remember getting on a call with a person who is an angel investor and is apparently connected with everyone in the world. "Something huge can happen from this!!!!" I thought. I wasn't trying to use him/her, but I figured that there was a great chance that this person would want to connect us to some other people. I was so excited and nervous as the call approached.

We got on the call, and I asked my normal questions trying to learn things from wealth of wisdom that this person had acquired. And after fifteen minutes there was not one question that came my way and the conversation ended. Nothing crazy happened. Sure I learned some things, but it did not result in a massive change in the trajectory of my life or our business.

I remember getting a trial with a professional soccer club thinking, "Great! Everything is about to change!" and then being completely underwhelmed when little in my life happened.

What I know is that I will have some great opportunities and meet some fantastic people leading up to October, but it is not who I meet or what happens that matters, it's who I am working on becoming. "October is coming Jamie, who do you want to be?"

There is a great chance that you have things in front of you that feel like insurmountable challenges. My encouragement to you is to look back and think of what you have been through in the past, what have you learned, and how life-altering was that challenge?

October is coming for all of us and I think one of the most beneficial things to do is to choose to move forward controlling controllables and focusing on who we want to become.

TRAIN To Be Clutch

- Pick a date that is a few months ahead.
- What do you have that is challenging in your mind between now and then?
- Imagine yourself at that date, reflecting back on how you handled those challenges. How do you hope you will have operated during that time?

They Are Always Learning. What Are We Modeling?

We strongly believe that the reason many teams never fulfill their potential is because they are trying to win instead of get better at every opportunity.

Every day we are presented with countless little choices: do I focus on how I look (winning) or do I focus on growth (getting better)?

If we focus on winning, we might win more games in the beginning, but the team that is focused on 1% growth everyday and cutting no corners will win way more in the long run.

You can cut corners to win, but those weaknesses will eventually come back to haunt you. We get so caught up on winning the moment that we aren't prepared for the future, and we sacrifice our potential at the altar of potentially winning.

If you take the short term view, "if we don't win, then we are all out of jobs" then you don't dismiss people from practice, you don't sit people out of games, you don't enforce healthy boundaries with love and respect because you are operating in short term survival mode.

The ironic part is that the graves of many head coaching positions are filled with people who took this approach. When you focus on winning and your uncontrollable outcome based goals you unknowingly erode the foundation of your program.

If you take the long term view, and you are focused on developing people for life after sports, and maximizing their potential, then it is simple to dismiss people from practice, sit them at games, and enforce healthy boundaries with love and respect. A leader with this view understands that no short-term gains are worth eroding the culture and character of the program.

When you are focused long-term, you know that deep learning and growing in the most important areas are what matter most. When you focus long-term you know that learning the fundamental lessons and principles upon which your program will be built are more important than any short-lived victory on the scoreboard.

If you focus on equipping people for the future and maximizing their potential you shift from *survive mode* to *thrive mode*. That doesn't guarantee you will win or even keep your job, but it does create a culture with the foundation necessary to sustain success.

Worst-case scenario, you lose your job, but you learn valuable lessons for the next opportunity for how to build a better foundation. Best-case scenario, when you focus on short term you never get out of survival mode and you are constantly trying to plug the holes and cracks and are constantly distracted from leading.

We don't know what the results will turn out to be. It's not a guarantee that focusing on the important things (long-term) won't produce short-term results. John Wooden said that though we may not like them, the results will probably be about where they should be if we focus on progress and growth.

The crux of the matter is *what will matter ten to twenty years from now?*

What we choose to focus on now is laying the foundation for the rest of their lives. They are always learning, but most of the time we are completely unaware of what we are modeling for them.

It's All About Getting High. We Are All Addicts.

You may have never taken a hit from a crack pipe, a puff from a joint, or awakened with a desperation to get high on meth, but I'm sure you have struggled. Chances are you still struggle; but with an even greater addiction:

The high of winning the game, the championship, the girl, or the sale.

We are addicted to the high of winning.

The problem is the same with winning as it is with hard drugs; you always need more to get that same high. For most of us it started with winning a game when we were on the playground or the YMCA league, and we have been addicts ever since.

But what happens if you win it all and you still feel empty inside? You don't have to look too hard to find that this is the case for many people in Hollywood and at the pinnacle of professional sports.

When we win we are on top of the world--at least for a moment--but when we lose, we are thrown into the throws of the deepest darkness.

If we are "a somebody" when we achieve our goals, who are we when we fail to achieve them?

Is our identity found in something that can be taken away from us in the blink of an eye?

Too many people are being used by their sport, vocation, and education. If we find our identity in what we do, or anything else that can be taken away from us, including our kids, it is a recipe for disaster.

Sports can be transformational. However, if our identity is found in winning, coaching, playing, or obtaining results, we are functional addicts who are most likely dying inside.

When my undergrad decided to cut the men's soccer program my life came to a halt. I ran out of the locker room and sat down in the dark at the soccer stadium crying as hard as I ever had to that point. Was I going to take the top-class education or try to transfer and play ball? Because of the timing, I thought all of my transfer options would have left me side-lined for a year. And I was hit with the question: "If I don't play soccer, who am I?" I realized at that moment that my identity was completely wrapped up in my sport. It was that moment when I truly decided to find my identity in Christ, something that could never be taken away from me.

So many people in athletics experience a painfully similar identity crisis when they finish playing after high school, college or pro, because for so long they have wrapped up their identity in how they kick, hit, or throw a ball.

Some experience the crisis and the emotional rollercoaster during their time in college or professional sports, because they go from being a big fish in a little pond, to a little fish in a big pond.

They experience depression, some even take their own lives.

When I ask people, "Who would you be if you lost the ability to play your sport?" They usually say something like, "I would be an actor," "I would be an artist," or "I would be a doctor." But I didn't ask them **what they would do**, I asked them **who they would be**. Being and doing are very different. Who are you outside of what you do? Who are you when everything is stripped away?

My friend Danny has struggled every morning for the last eight years. He wakes up fighting the urge to stick a heroin needle in his veins. Danny is a very athletic looking guy, and upon first glance I would have never guessed he battles a heroin addiction. He looks more like someone playing professional sports than a person addicted to heroin. He asked me to share his story because after he finished college baseball he had an identity crisis, and he needed to fill the addiction winning had given him, so he turned to drugs.

Make sure you value people, way above and beyond performance. In fact, maybe we shouldn't refer to the people on our team as athletes, point guards, midfielders, or pitchers. These only serve as labels that people use to find their identity. If and when their sport is finished or is taken away, what have we set them up to believe about themselves?

As a person who plays, make sure you find your identity in something that can never be taken away from you.

You didn't get into God's family because of your performance, and you won't get kicked out because of your performance. God chose to love you because of who He is, not because of who you are or what you did, so He's not going to stop loving you. –Judah Smith

TRAIN To Be Clutch

- Where do you find your identity?
- Do people in your hometown know you as a basketball player, a golfer, soccer player, actress, consultant, writer,

CEO, pastor, coach, or musician? If so, what happens if you lose your ability to participate in those contexts?

- Listen to how people are talked about on tv, in the news, and even in the conversations of those you are around most. Do they equate someone's identity with what they do?

- When someone asks you what you do, tell them about things you enjoy doing instead of your profession or education.

- I wonder what it would look like if we stopped asking people what they do for a living, and we started answering that question with what we are passionate about?!

- PLEASE stop asking people what they do. Ask them what makes their heart sing. Ask them what they are passionate about.

It Has To Be YOUR Dream!

I've yelled this many times in speaking engagements to young people, but I think I'm going to have to start focusing even more on it. In this age of "helicopter parents" and people in leadership roles telling 8 year olds they need to specialize in one sport, I'm not sure how many kids even know whose dream they are pursuing. They are being pushed to pursue someone else's dream and usually by someone who didn't achieve their own. I find it interesting that Archie Manning wouldn't let Peyton or Eli play football until high school; he never pushed them and they seemed to have done just fine at their sport and in life.

Recently I was having a conversation with an incredibly bright and relatively successful person who served as an assistant coach at a top university. She is doing our reading challenge (available at the back of the book and on the homepage of t2bc.com) and she just finished one of our highest recommended books, "Mindset." As we were discussing her challenges, I told her a story.

We were doing a drill where the people on our team were supposed to be yelling, "BALL, BALL, BALL" as they did slides across the lane. During one of the breaks, I went up to one of the girls and I said, "You want to do public speaking, right?" She said, "Yeah, I think so." I said, "Cool, the thing about public speaking is that you have to over-communicate, be a little dramatic, and much louder than feels comfortable. So this is an excellent opportunity to develop that skill in this drill."

Very simple. Nothing profound. I just connected a mundane drill to her developing the skills which will greatly benefit her in her dream job.

But here is the thing, I had to know what HER DREAM was to be able to do that.

After I told the person coaching this story and told her about the importance of asking people "what is your dream?" she confessed that she couldn't remember a person who coached her *EVER* asking her that question.

Many people who play begin to question whether they are wasting their time with their sport when they have the realization they are most likely not going to play at the next level. This realization can lead to a dramatic shift in effort and care for developing their skills. This is where it is **YOUR RESPONSIBILITY** to connect the dots for them, **BUT** you have to know what *their* dream is.

Here are some examples:

You want to be a neurosurgeon? As a neurosurgeon you might be in surgery for up to 20 hours and need meticulous focus and precision WITH SOMEONE'S LIFE ON THE LINE. We are asking you to focus for around 3-5 hours for practice or competition, and no ones life is on the line.

You want to be a mom and serve as an executive? You are going to have to be able to juggle and compartmentalize a lot of things in life. Therefore, learning how to come to practice and focus, even when you have a test the next day, is preparing you for the next stages of your life.

You want to serve as the C.E.O. of a Fortune 500 company? You are going to have to learn how to work with people you don't like. You may not like all of your teammates, but if you can serve them and help them be better everyday, you are training yourself to be better serving as a C.E.O.

You want to serve as a surgeon? Sometimes you are going to be called in at 3 o'clock in the morning to do surgery on someone and their life might depend on you being at your best even though you haven't gotten a lot of sleep. So, I understand you were up all night studying for an exam, but doing these seemingly mundane drills right now is a great training exercise for you fulfilling your dream perfroming surgeries.

These examples might seem like common sense to you and I, and you can probably think of hundreds of better examples. However, *I hear people in coaching talk about how sports are a great training ground for life, but I rarely hear the people coaching actually teach these examples on the day to day.* Most of the time their explanations have to do with how something connects back to golf, basketball, soccer, or whatever sport they play. The connections to real life are rarely taught.

This is very dangerous because you then put fuel on the fire for some of the people on your team to believe all *you* actually care about is *your* own personal livelihood. And on a serious note, they might be right. If you never stop and become fully present to ask the person on your team, "What is your dream?" how can you say your mission is to train and equip them for life?

If they know we care about their dreams and are invested in helping them achieve them, they will tap into reservoirs of persistence, courage, and passion you never knew existed.

This is also why it is so important you burn your goals and focus on developing true mental toughness, because then it isn't about winning or losing a mostly inconsequential game; rather, it is about becoming the type of people we want to be.

Move towards transformational leadership by investing quality time with your kids to know what their dreams are, and figure out how you can use your sport to help them become the type of person who has the best chance of achieving those dreams.

TRAIN To Be Clutch

- If you are in leadership, do you know what the dreams are of the people on your team?
- Are you making a consistent effort to help the people on your team pursue *their* dreams?
- If you are the one playing or working, have you taken the time to think about what YOUR dream really is?
- Are you in the process of chasing someone else's dream for you?
- What is your dream? It's got to be YOUR dream, YOUR vision for your life. Once you know that, then we can send you out full steam ahead with strategies and tools that will help you move toward fulfilling your potential. But if you don't know that, or if you have a whole bunch of conflicting beliefs or values, then you will become your own worst enemy.

CHAPTER

Everything Matters.
Everyone Matters.

A number of years ago an elderly couple wandered into a small hotel in downtown Philadelphia. It was 1am in the morning, pouring down rain and they desperately needed a room. The young clerk said there were no rooms available, and in fact there was a convention in town and there wasn't a room in the entire city of Philadelphia.

He said, "But I can't send you away. I have a staff room here in the back that you can sleep in. You can shower and rest up and stay warm." The couple resisted, not wanting to be a burden, but the young clerk insisted they stay. So they showered, slept, and in the morning they thanked him for his kindness.

"You ought to be the manager of the finest hotel in the world!" The older man said. Then they packed up the car and went on their way.

About 2 years later the young clerk received a letter from a name unfamiliar to him. Inside was an invitation to visit NY and paid round-trip ticket. So he packed up his bags and went. A driver collected him from the airport and took him to 5th and 34th street and there was a brand new building rising into the sky. He got out of the car and the elderly man from that night stuck his hand out to introduce himself and said, "In case you don't remember me, my name is William Waldorf Aster and this is our very first Waldorf Astoria Hotel. William Bolt, I want you to be its manager."

What it would look like if we treated every person, client, and opportunity if it was our dream opportunity?

When I wake up in the morning I try to approach everything I do with this heart. When I go to the gym and interact with people I pass, when I go to check out at the grocery store, when I interact on twitter or speak with auditoriums filled with people, I try to operate with passion and heart. I am trying to treat people better than I *think* they deserve to be treated. I am trying to treat people like I want to be treated. I am trying to treat people according to the vision of who I believe they can become. And I will be the first to say that I am not perfect.

I don't know what you are going through right now. I don't know what kind of menial tasks you have lined up for today. I have no idea how things are going to pan out for you. But I do know everything matters and everyone matters.

Jackie Robinson never knew all the harassment and trials he went through growing up were preparing him for his destiny. We never know, and we can never know how many opportunities have unknowingly slipped through our fingers. If William Bolt had turned away those guests on a rainy night, he would have never known the opportunity that slipped away.

What would your world look like if up to this point you believed everything and everyone matters?

What could happen to your game if you believed every rep and every possession mattered?

What could happen in your life if you believed every person you get to coach was just as valuable as Kevin Durant or LeBron James?

My hope is I would treat every opportunity as if it was the opportunity of my dreams.

TRAIN To Be Clutch

- What are some of the more mundane situations in your day? How are those contexts opportunities to train who you are becoming?
- What is not asked of you in your job or team? Can you still choose to be excellent?

The Future Of Leadership Is Treating People Like People

When I first moved to Los Angeles and I was flat broke one of my friends at that time bought me a pair of shoes from Nordstrom.

I loved these shoes and I wore them every day and everywhere for four months. After four months these shoes were filthy from my days spent loading and delivering food around the most impoverished areas of the city and my nights spent exploring the city.

These shoes were on their last leg, and I asked my friend if she had the receipt. She gave it to me and I tried to take them back to Nordstrom.

Sure enough, they gave me cash for the shoes, with a smile on their face. I couldn't believe it! I went to Nordstrom rack and bought two new pairs with the money from my refund.

I was broke and I took advantage of the system.

Fast forward to today. I make very good money, and guess where I love to shop?

Nordstrom.

I am not afraid to spend $500 on a pair of boots because I know if anything goes wrong, I have full confidence Nordstrom will make it right. By allowing me the opportunity to take advantage of the system they now benefit from the lifetime value of my loyalty not only as a customer, but also as a brand ambassador.

With how much money businesses pay on marketing I wonder how many raving fans and brand ambassadors they miss out on because they worry about missing out on tiny revenues. Businesses trip over dollars trying to pickup pennies, meanwhile big businesses flush millions of dollars down the toilet trying to get new customers that would actually be influenced by their friends and family if the business actually cared about them and treated them like people.

How many times do businesses suffer because they are "just trying to make money." Instead of provide a useful service or product.

How many times do they miss out on incredible revenue because of shortsighted decisions that place short-term revenues over long term impact.

If you focus on building an incredible product that meets real needs, then the money will follow. If you focus on creating a product that just makes money, you will miss a lot of opportunities to build great products and services that stand the test of time.

I wonder how many people in coaching undercut their program by narrowing the majority of their focus on the new people they want on their team? Do they really care about the *person* they are recruiting or just the recruit that signs on the line? How do you treat those who are on your team and the ones that tell you no after many months of recruiting and traveling? Are they a person or a production unit?

The future of leadership is treating people like people. Putting first things first scares a lot of people in business, because they are worried about change and being taken advantage of.

Businesses cried aghast when child labor laws made it illegal for children to work in factories and more expensive labor cut into their margins.

Business once again cried out in backlash to "green initiatives" and pushed back against cleaning up emissions that were poisoning air and water quality because they thought it would drop the bottom line.

When New York City moved to smokeless bars businesses experts once again cried wolf, claiming an entire industry would once again die.

No one could imagine that a company like Nordstom could survive by taking back anything, no matter what, including things like tires they never sold. And the critics were correct, they didn't survive, they actually thrived.

I love how Seth Godin puts it: "It often seems like standing up for dignity, humanity and respect for those without as much power is called anti-business. And yet it turns out that the long-term benefit for businesses is that they are able to operate in a more stable, civilized, sophisticated marketplace. It's pretty easy to go back to a completely self-regulated, selfishly focused, Ayn-Randian cut-throat short-term world. But I don't think you'd want to live there."

Put first things first in business, sports, and life, and the secondary things will get better as well! When people treat people like people, there will always be progress and growth!

It's Only A PART Of The Story

I didn't want to go there, and I wasn't sure if I should have. It's easy to connect with people over tragedy. You can tell people about the toughest things you have been through in life, and more often than not you will create a deeper connection with them.

I have seen it work. I've studied the principles in psychology. I spent a significant amount of my life connecting with people through my pain.

I hate to do it now.

But I did. I was speaking to a group of young adults who had gone through a really tough situation, and I shared the tragedies of my life to make sure I connected with them. I was scared and didn't want them to think I was some privileged kid who had never been through anything.

It worked.

Some might have said it worked exceptionally well.

Yet, I still didn't feel comfortable about having done it. I was talking to my mom later that day, and I told her I had told them about all the bad stuff that happened in my childhood.

She said, "Joshua, it's ok, it's YOUR story."

And that's when it hit me, it is not **MY** story. It is *a part* of my story, but it is not *THE* story.

I lived for a long time under that victim mentality and the bondage of those negative events in my life.

But I have a future and a hope, and that is only A PART of the story.

When we make the tragedies and awful things that happen in our lives THE story, we enslave ourselves to those circumstances. We keep ourselves in bondage to those events as we continually think about them and share them with others.

I believe there is someone who loves me unconditionally who came to give us a new story, a future and a hope. I choose to believe tragedies are only a part of our story.

TRAIN To Be Clutch

- In an effort to legitimize all the struggles I had been through as a child I actually repressed many of the good memories and it took years of work before I recovered them.
- We all have a story, and all of us have been through crazy stuff. What have you been holding onto as YOUR story that is only a part of the story?
- List out 5 awesome experiences that you *did* get to enjoy throughout the course of your life.
- Try writing down 3-15 amazing blessings that you have right now in your life each morning for the next three days.
- Remember, we get more of what we look for.

This Is Where The Goodness Happens

It rarely fails that when someone reaches out they want me to help them eradicate fear in their life. I quickly tell them that the complete eradication of fear, in my opinion, is not possible, and it's not helpful.

When our brain shoots off a signal that a social situation has turned and could result in violence, fear is a good thing. When there is a grizzly bear coming towards you, fear is a good thing. It means RUN!!!!!

The thing with fear is that too many of us see it as a problem rather than seeing it as a signal.

When I was in college the most dreaded fitness test was the beep test. You had to run from one cone to the next and then back again making sure that you touched every cone before the beep from the CD player went off. The beeps started getting closer and closer meaning that you had to run harder the more tired you got. You don't pass the beep test. You run until failure. "Fun" is not exactly the word that comes to mind!

Every time I heard that the beep test was coming, my mind would fill with fear and dread. I never once went into that test believing that it was the best thing for me. That distinctive beep became the signal that induced trepidation.

At that time in my life I did not think about how going through the hardest runs would be the best thing for me. I had crazy dreams in soccer and going through runs like the beep test was essential for my growth and development. Really, the beep test should have been a signal for me saying, "Jamie, this is where the goodness happens."

The other day I walked into a ballroom with tables set up for a banquet. As I walked in I saw a flyer laying out the agenda for the night with a huge picture of my face, "Jamie Gilbert – Keynote Speaker." This flyer was on every single one of the place settings for 1,000 people that were soon to fill the room. My heart started pounding!

As I was sitting with the guy who serves as the president of the university, I was wondering, "Jamie, what are you doing here? Why would they want to listen to you? You are a fraud and everyone is about to find out!!"

About midway through the banquet I glanced at the agenda and saw that I only had a few people left in front of me. My fear scepter was going bonkers! It was one of those moments when you can feel your heart pounding out of your neck! I glanced once more at the bottom of the agenda and it said "Keynote Speaker – Jamie Gilbert." There was nothing left on the page.

Now as my heart rate increased, my training kicked in. The signal that has so often told me "Jamie, give up! You can't do this!" changed its tune.

I simply smiled to myself and said "Jamie, this is where the goodness happens!"

I started with regulating my heart rate. It's something I have practiced in the past many times by intentionally breathing in for 4 seconds, pausing for 1 second, and exhaling for 5 seconds. I did that six times, which drastically reduced my heart rate.

During that time, I decided to glance at my notes. All I wanted to see was the first fifteen seconds of what I was going to say, because I knew if I had the first few seconds down, my training would take over and I would deliver well from there on.

I thought for a second about what I was likely to do if I let anxiety and emotions get the best of me. I would either stumble with my first few words or try to tell a joke. Jokes usually don't work well for me and stumbling in the first few words usually creates more nervousness.

So once I saw myself going through how I *didn't* want to handle things, I then began to see myself communicating the way that I wanted to. I got up there, paused with a smile, and then began.

I'll admit that it wasn't **THE** best talk I've given, but it was much better than what would have happened if I focused on all the fear and anxiety that I was feeling. More importantly, that talk became a training ground for me to reframe fear in my life. Since that talk my dominant phrase when fear creeps in is "Jamie, this is where the goodness happens."

Again, it is not the complete eradication of fear that we are shooting for. It's developing the mindset of being willing to embrace things that unnerve us. Its reframing the alarm bells in our minds that traditionally move us towards dwelling on things outside of our control, and coming back to controlling the controllables.

Fear does not have to be our foe. Fear can be our friend that tells us *"This is where the goodness happens."*

TRAIN To Be Clutch

- What are some reoccurring situations where you feel resistance and fear welling up?
- How are those situations actually opportunities for you to grow?
- What can you choose to believe when you feel the fear signal going off?
- You can start with small things or jump into giant fears, but making a start at reframing that signal could radically alter the generations to come!

The Path To Mastery

"What brings you to Missouri?" asked the young man working at the car rental agency. I told him I was in town to do a workshop with Mizzou Women's basketball. He went on to explain how he used to play competitive hockey growing up. I asked him what happened with it, and this was his exact response: "Mannnn, that shit started to take over my life. I was traveling every weekend, and I had no life, so I quit."

Now, the ironic part of this story was that two years before in an interview with *Enterprise* rent a car, I was told I wasn't qualified to be a rental car agent with their company.

BUT that is a story for another day, and I digress.

Maybe this young man dreamed of working at a car rental car agency, but I have a sneaking suspicion he was not working at his dream job. But working there had taken over his life.

I doubt anyone had explained the path to mastery, as George Leonard lays out in his book, *Mastery.*

The path to mastery isn't complicated as you can see from the picture, and in fact it is quite simple. You have a short growth spurt, followed by a slight dip, and then a long plateau. This same pattern plays out OVER and OVER and OVER and OVER and OVER again.

Where do you think most people quit?

They quit on the plateau, because they feel like all their hard work is no longer paying off and is a waste of their time.

But what you will find over and over again when studying people who have done great things is that they share a similar perspective to Thomas Edison: "I haven't failed, I've just found ten thousand ways that won't work."

He was committed to the path to mastery, as are so many professionals in different areas of life.

Plateaus are inevitable, even for those who are the best in the world at their craft. This is why it is even more important to fall in love with the process of becoming great rather than goals and results. We can't control results, and we are going to hit plateaus. It is easier to push through the plateaus when we love the journey not just the results. You will also find many people who have made the most money, and who create the best work, do things they are passionate about, not for the money or the accolades. Mark Zuckerberg, Mother Teresa, and Steve Jobs are three of the best examples.

The beautiful thing about the path to mastery is that if you know you are getting great coaching, and you are putting in the hard work and long hours, you can have peace that you are on the path to mastery EVEN when you are not getting any better for long periods of time. The only thing you shouldn't do is QUIT.

Let's be clear about some things:

Does the path to mastery apply to people in coaching? YES

Does the path to mastery apply to people in school? YES

Does the path to mastery apply to teams? YES

Does the path to mastery apply to businesses? YES

It is easy to throw in the towel and abandon your strategy of loving, encouraging, and holding high standards with your team when it feels like you have been doing it for months but it feels like you aren't getting anywhere.

Keep the faith!

There are plenty of people who have come before and shown the strategy works, so just keep persevering and stay on the path to mastery!

This is what we tell our kids to do, right? If they came to us after a few months and said, I've been doing EVERYTHING you asked me to do....

I watch extra film.

I put in hours of extra training on my own every week.

I read transformational books.

I spend time every week on mental training.

AND I'M STILL NOT SEEING THE RESULTS IN COMPETITION!!!

We would all give them the same advice: "Just trust me, keep doing it, and it is GOING TO PAY OFF".

The path to mastery is the same for all of us in all facets of life. **Be encouraged and persevere when you hit the plateaus because you know you are on the path to mastery. Explain it to your team, and most importantly, *MODEL* it for them in everything you do.**

Most people are going to quit on a plateau or a dip, but it will be the ones who persevere, OVER and OVER and OVER and OVER again, who will succeed.

The guy working at the rental car agency was right, **something** is going to take over your life, don't you want it to be something you are extremely passionate about??

I've learned that no matter who you are or how "talented" you think you are, you can never skip plateaus, you can only embrace them as a part of the journey to the elusive concept of mastery.

Now that we know what the path to mastery looks like, we will examine the road signs on the path to mastery.

CHAPTER

Road Signs on the Path to Mastery

Earlier this year I was driving my mother-in-law's car from Denver to Nashville where she now lives. It's about an eighteen-hour drive I split up by a pit stop in Tulsa to see my family. The second day of my trip was nine hours on I-40 east. I was about seven hours into the drive and completely engulfed in the audiobook, *In A Pit With A Lion On A Snowy Day*. All of a sudden, I sort of snapped out of my trance, and a paralyzing thought hit me: "Am I still on the right road?"

For the last three hours I hadn't stopped for food, gas or to use the restroom. I had not detoured or switched highways, but the thought had me worried.

"Am I going in the right direction?"

I was finally put to ease when I saw that little blue sign that said I-40 and a subsequent mile-marker that showed how far I was from Nashville.

What's interesting is that the same thing happens with people in their sport, teams, business, corporations, and those who are investing in their child's development (a.k.a. parents who stay-at-home to raise their child). The road signs on the path to mastery are similar regardless of the context we find ourselves in at any particular time in life. We can take solace in knowing that we are going in the right direction by the signs on the road. Here are some of those road signs:

- This is hard.
- I don't *feel* like doing _____ today.
- Everyone else has more time than me.
- I don't *feel* like this is making a difference.
- Almost no one else is doing this.

Sound familiar?

Kevin Durant puts himself through the hardest training in the off-season having someone deliberately hit him, slap him, and push him as he shoots and drives to the basket. The hard stuff is what has him leading the league in and-1's and free throws.

We played division 1 sport alongside someone who sits at the top of the world golf rankings. We hardly ever saw him on campus because he was always at the course grinding on his craft. His studies and his practice left him little time for hanging out with the guys.

When we first started to reach out to people on Twitter and provide them with videos and other tools, it felt like it wasn't making a difference. Many people told us to "F*$* off" "Eat #$$% and die. QUIT SPAMMING!" Waking up to those @ mentions isn't the most pleasant experience in the world. We experienced that for over 6 months before everything really took off.

It felt foolish to be the only two people on campus training from 11 PM until 1 AM on Friday and Saturday nights, especially when you know everyone else is out having a good time. After we saw the impact deliberate practice had on our game after a summer playing with some of the best in college soccer, this was how we spent many weekend nights during the offseason.

The thing about all of these signs is that they provide information but they don't give a whole lot of instruction. They are the square signs like mile-markers and rest stop options that tell us where things are. But the great thing about most highways is that they don't just provide *information*; they actually provide *instruction* that will help us move safely and efficiently towards our destination. These are the yellow diamond signs that we see instructing us about speed change for a sharp bend, uneven roads, or roadwork ahead. The road signs on the path to mastery are no different. So what are some of the path to mastery's instructions?

- Talk to yourself instead of listening to yourself.
- Ask the question, "What is one thing I can do to make the situation better?" Rather than, "why is this happening to me?"
- Live by principles rather than feelings.

*We will discuss each of these in the next three chapters.

Finally there are warning signs that mark the path. They are signs that warn us about the result of our choices. On the highway we see things like fines double in the work zone, $1,000 fine for littering, and HOV violators maximum fine $500. They are the boundaries that we must operate in or else there will be a consequence. The path to mastery is marked with those as well.

- Your choice creates your challenge
- You are building your own house
- Your choice creates a challenge for those on your team
- You will reap what you sow
- The grass is greener where you water it
- The wise man finds the diamonds on his own land

Even though the path to mastery is available to everyone, very few will choose to take it.

Will there be obstacles? Yes.

Will there be people who try to hold you back? Yes.
Will there be circumstances that create challenges outside of your control? Yes.
Will it be lonely at times? Yes.

But choosing to believe that anything that happens is in your best interest will turn all of the challenges and circumstances into a refinery that will shape your character, skills, and ability to change the world.

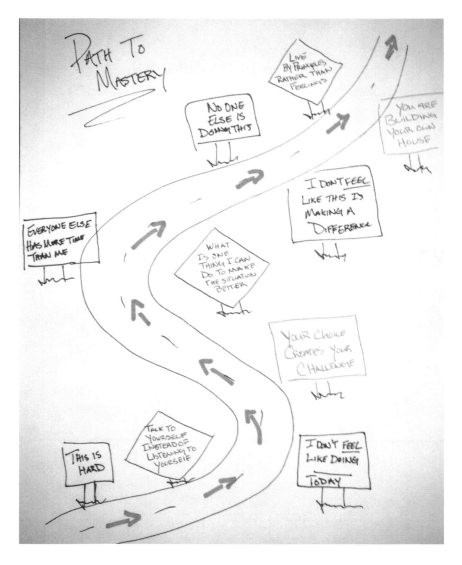

It Won't Be Easy. It Will Be Worth It.

My flight is supposed to board in 5 minutes and I sent Jamie this text message, "I'm seriously fighting the urge to walk out of the airport and not go speak."

I had just read intake forms from the young women I was supposed to be speaking to in less than 6 hours, and I was disgusted. The day before I was told that the lady who serves as the sport psychologist at their university claimed it would be a "high risk" for the administration to allow me to meet individually with the ladies because I am not a "certified" psychologist. From reading the intake forms it was obvious the young women were DESPERATE for help from someone who was qualified to help them, and this lady was clearly failing them miserably in this regard. AND NOW she was attempting to stand in the way of them getting the help from me that they needed.

The thoughts reverberating around my head were nearing dangerous speeds and none of them were helpful.

"I'm the best in the world at what I do, and my track record shows it. Who does this pathetic sport psychologist think she is?"

"How ignorant are you to not call the people who have me on their staff, who allow me to meet individually with the people on their team on a weekly basis, and ask about my track record?!"

"Why should I even go on this trip?! I can drive to Cal and Stanford tomorrow and be there to support the girls and the program who want me to be there."

"Fear and ignorance are pathetic!"

And there were MANY more thoughts along the same lines.

I could quite literally feel my blood pressure rising and I was ready to explode.

As I sat at gate 1 in the Southwest terminal at LAX, I was getting ready to walk out of the airport and catch a cab home when a thought popped into my mind:

"Are you listening to yourself or are you talking to yourself??"

I knew I was listening to myself and I knew how destructive it could be if I didn't stop listening and start talking to myself. I went into the bathroom and I started speaking my mission for myself over my life and into the mirror.

"Your mission is to transform hearts and minds through love and mentorship. Your mission is to transform hearts and minds through love and mentorship. Your mission is to transform hearts and minds through love and mentorship. Trust in the lord with all your heart, lean not on your own understanding, in all your ways acknowledge Him and He will direct your paths. Have I not commanded you? Be strong and courageous; do not be afraid, for the Lord your God will be with you, wherever you will go."

"What an opportunity?! This is in your best interest and an opportunity to learn and grow. You want to make these girls feel loved and valued

unconditionally for who they are as people. Are you operating out of fear or love? Are you making this about YOU or THEM?"

"Check your ego at the door. Have a great attitude. Give your very, very best. Treat people really, really well. Have unconditional gratitude. REGARDLESS of your circumstances."

"This story is going to impact thousands of lives down the road. Sometimes you have to say F your feelings and act like the person you want to become. This problem is standing between you and your dreams. Are you going to run from this 500 pound lion, or are you going to chase it into a pit on a snowy day and kill it? Strength is only built through resistance. You have an opportunity to change the trajectory of people's lives."

I got on the plane and, even though I still wasn't ecstatic about the trip, I believed I was being intentional rather than reactionary. I believed I was making the most beneficial choice from the options I had in front of me. I had talked to myself instead of listening to myself.

On the plane I listened to 2 songs on repeat for the entire 4 hour flight. *Use the pain*, by Eric Thomas, and *Trust in Jesus*, by Third Day.

I gave the workshop, and even though it probably wasn't the best I've ever done, I did my best. Over the next few days, many of the girls on the team chose to meet with me based on their own accord, and four out of six of them used the phrase "life-changing" to describe the meeting.

Sometimes when we teach principles like talk to yourself vs. listen to yourself, I think people think it is easy for us. Sometimes I think people think these things come naturally to us.

They don't.

It is hard, sometimes excruciatingly hard.
Sometimes we don't make the most beneficial choice.
We are on this journey as well.

I want to encourage you. The next time you find yourself ready to explode ask yourself this question:

Am I listening to myself or talking to myself?

The next time you feel like you have nothing left in the tank, ask yourself are you listening to yourself, or talking to yourself?

It won't be easy....
It will be worth it....

Sometimes we have to save F our feelings and act like the person we want to become.

TRAIN To Be Clutch

- While we cannot control the thoughts that come into our heads, we can choose whether or not we entertain them.
- At the end of your meeting, training, or at the end of the day, evaluate the things you said to yourself. When did you listen to yourself and when did you talk to yourself?
- Remember that when training your self-talk, we need to continually become aware of what we are saying and become intentional about changing it. It's a *process!*

I'm A Fake. I'm A Fraud. It's Only A Matter Of Time Before Everyone Finds Out.

From a very young age I can remember having this feeling that I didn't really belong.

Do you ever feel like a fake?
Do you ever feel like a fraud?
Maybe you wonder why people should even listen to you or follow you?

I know that as I reflect on the influence we have on people, I often wonder why any of these people, some of whom operate at the very top of their craft, should take the wisdom from the things I have studied and experienced and alter their work, relationships, game, and life around those principles.

One day I was out at one of the nicest golf courses in the world with my friend who caddies on tour and my other friend who plays on the PGA tour when I was hit with this doubt storm.

"Jamie, what are you doing just standing here? Do something valuable!!!"

"Jamie, what is he even bringing you along for? Why is he paying you?"

The waves of doubt really started to rock the boat when there was another guy who was working with him on his short game. It was as if those two were the only ones on the green. Doubt after doubt kept hitting me, each time cutting deeper and deeper. I felt like I should say something, but I didn't want to sound like an idiot and stumble.

"Jamie, what do you know about the putting stroke? How are you going to provide value???"

I finally started to muster up the courage to say something, but as it was about to pour out of my mouth something hit me: "Jamie, don't just talk to say something. Say something that needs to be heard, but don't just talk to try and be significant."

So I said nothing.

As we were walking the course I kept pretty quiet, but internally I kept saying "Jamie, provide some value!!!"

As I was about to speak a verse hit me on number 6. "Humble yourself before the Lord and He will exalt you." James 4:10

That shut me up really quick, but it also reminded me that I am not alone. There is purpose to my existence. There is purpose to my presence on that course with those three guys. I'm not inadequate. I am a child of the immaculate! I am here for a reason, but don't just try to blow things up yourself. Wait for the Lord and He will exalt you!

So I said nothing audibly, but internally, the chatter began to lessen. I had a clearer focus as I watched these guys work and prepare.

After the round, we all went to the practice green and he began practicing putts. Watching him tinker with his stroke and grow more and more frustrated, I stepped in. I had something valuable to say. Something that I knew from experience and my area of expertise. So I jumped in and said, "You're done man. Let's go home. You're going to try and find something to fix. You're good."

He looked up at me, smiled and agreed. Home we went.

What I know is that for a long time in my life I have questioned whether or not I provide value. When I was training with a professional soccer club, I questioned whether or not I belonged. I would look at the guys around me and draw the conclusion that these guys were *born for this*, but me, I'm a fake trying to make it. And in those times it is extremely hard to objectively look at the evidence for those beliefs because the evidence seems etched in stone.

What I know is that those thoughts and feelings never seem to go away completely. But the more I intentionally remind myself of who God is and who He says I am, the less those attacks have an adverse effect on my life.

Maybe you don't feel like you belong. The others in your industry or sport were groomed for this, but you, you're just there by luck and it's only a matter of time before everyone finds out and they get rid of you.

What you and I need to reflect on is that we can have the confidence *of* Jesus because of our confidence *in* Jesus.

First of all, what is the confidence of Jesus?

Jesus did some crazy things and did a lot of things that unnerved people. A crowd backed him to the edge of a cliff and he looked at them and just walked past them. But the craziest thing he did was stoop down and wash the disciples' feet.

That takes confidence. But his confidence was never conjured up. It came from a firm belief and foundation in something that never changes.

In John 13 we find Jesus in a small room with his closest followers, and it is here that the source of his confidence unfolds. It says:

Jesus, knowing that the Father had given all things into his hands, and that he had come from God and was going back to God, rose from supper. He laid aside his outer garments, and taking a towel, tied it around his waist. Then he poured water into a basin and began to wash the disciples' feet.

When we know *who* made us and we know that the end of the matter is already settled, that allows us to do some radical stuff!

Now, it can lead to some pride and arrogance, which it did for some of the early Christians and plenty of believers today. But ultimately I believe it leads us to humility. **Humility isn't believing that we are weak and have nothing to provide. It's believing that we have nothing to prove, and many to love.**

As we engage with people who operate at the highest levels in the PGA, NBA, MLS, MLB, LPGA, NFL, college coaching, and at the highest levels in business, we have realized that we all have one thing in common: At times we all feel like we don't belong. **And just knowing that we all struggle with similar challenges should give us the comfort and freedom to move forward embracing the feelings of inadequacy.**

Here is my advice to you:

Embrace the fear. Do it scared. Humble yourself. Don't blow yourself up!

It's a daily challenge that I face and I know others face across the board. But know this, we can have the confidence *of* Jesus because of our confidence *in* Jesus.

If you don't know Him and would like to, email Jamie@ traintobeclutch.com or Joshua@traintobeclutch.com and we would love to walk alongside you in that journey.

TRAIN To Be Clutch

- What are the dominant contexts in your life where you feel inadequate?
- What are the dominant thoughts that run through your head?
- Write out three phrases you can say to yourself when those thoughts flood your mind.

EVERYTHING Has Hit The Fan!

At the beginning of this season one of the girls on the team I get to work with tore her ACL. Everyone in her life was telling her how sorry they were and treating her like she lost a parent.

I'm sure most of these people were coming from a good place, but I don't think that is the most beneficial thing to do. **Many times in life we experience trials that are outside of our control and the most dangerous thing we can do is feel sorry for ourselves and become immobilized.**

The first day I saw her, I gave her a big hug and told her how excited I was and that she had an amazing opportunity to learn and grow. **The next thing I asked her to do was create a "Can Do" list**. A list of ALL the things she could do to get better while she was recovering.

It is easy to slip into depression, feel sorry for yourself, and focus on all the things you can't do. Creating and using a "Can Do" list helps fight this disease.

People are watching how you handle yourself in this trial, and they will learn more about you from how you handle adversity then anything else. Gold is refined in the fire, diamonds are formed under pressure, but most of us run and hide every time we have an opportunity to be refined.

Don't get it twisted. This isn't just positive thinking. This is spending our energy constructively by focusing on the things inside of our control and embracing a growth mindset. **I don't have to know why things happen in my life. I don't have control over everything that happens to me. But I do have a choice over what I'm going to believe about it and what I'm going to do in THIS moment.**

What would it look like if we all started choosing to believe everything that happened to us is in our best interest and an opportunity to learn and grow?

Life will punch you in the face, it's a guarantee. You will lose loved ones, you will go through crazy trials, and you CAN let them define you or you can use them to refine you.

No matter what you are going through, trust Him, and direct all your focus on what you can do to get better in spite of your limiting circumstances. Remember, someone has had less and done more, and many people have had more and done less. It's not about what you have; it's about what you do with what you have.

TRAIN To Be Clutch

- What is your "Can Do" list for today? Writing this out each day is extremely powerful!
- Think back to an event or season in your life where you wish you had done things differently. How would you approach that situation now? Chances are there will be a similar situation in the near future.

Living By Principles vs. Living By Feelings

"At the end of your feelings is nothing. But at the end of every principle is a promise." –Eric Thomas

One day I was at a golf tournament and on the 18th green I was talking with one of the people competing in the tournament. I was explaining some of our *Train to be CLUTCH* principles and at one point she started trying to engage me in a philosophical debate. We hear this all the time and we have learned a quick question that cuts right to the heart of the matter. I asked, "How is that working out for you? How is your strategy of living by your feelings working out for you?"

Silence....and her head dropped.

"It's not working out very well."

She isn't alone. Living by our feelings is never going to workout very well for anyone. Feelings change. Sometimes we wakeup and we feel differently. Sometimes someone does something to make us feel differently. Living by our feelings is a rollercoaster.

When we make the choice to live by a certain set of principles it will not only protect us from our feelings, it will allow us to step into our greatest potential.

Many days we aren't going to feel like working out and honing our craft.
Many days we aren't going to feel like treating people really really well.
Many days we aren't going to feel like being unconditionally grateful.
Many days we aren't going to feel like giving our very best.

But the principle says you are going to reap what you sow.
The principle says those who are diligent workers are going to serve kings instead of mere men.
The principle says to turn the other cheek.
The principle says to seek wise counsel.
The principle says to speak life and not death.

At the end of our principles there is life, freedom, hope, joy, and peace.

At the end of our feelings is destruction.

Seek out the principles from ancient wisdom that have been tried and tested through the ages. When you switch from living by your feelings to living by principles, you will start to see very different fruit in your life. It isn't easy and sometimes we will slip up and make choices based off of our feelings. Pick yourself up, dust yourself off, and get back on the road to living by your principles rather than your feelings.

It's not easy, but it is more than worth it!

TRAIN To Be Clutch

- As you are reading the remainder of the book, write down principles that you would like to live your life by.
- When you wake up, before you enter the meeting, or before you play, write out 4-16 principles that you want to stick to no matter how crazy the situation gets.

Adopting A Growth Mindset Hurts

I tell people all the time that you do not just wake up one day with a Growth Mindset and never look back. It's something that is being developed over and over again every single day, and it is easy to slip in and out of a growth mindset. That being said, there are some pivotal moments where our mindset is intensely tested. This is one of the moments where my growth mindset was ruthlessly tested.

I had been training with a professional soccer team for about 3 months. I wasn't under contract. I wasn't getting much feedback from the team or staff. But I was trying so hard to learn and grow.

One day we went to the field for an inner-squad match. There were twenty-four people at training. The game was eleven vs. eleven so that left a remainder of two: me and a sixteen year-old kid named Brian.

So the game kicked off and I picked a player to watch and study. About five minutes in, one of the guys who was likely to start in the upcoming game rolled his ankle and had to come of. "Here's my chance!" I thought.

I started getting loose on the sidelines waiting for my name to be called. From the other side of the field, one of the guys coaching yelled, "Hey Brian, jump on the yellows."

Immediately, my heart sank. I could see a few guys who were on the field and closest to me try to cover their faces as they laughed at me.

It wasn't the ideal situation in my mind. I had played division 1 soccer and played overseas, I was ten years older, and Brian was five foot six inches, one hundred and twenty pounds, and got a hall pass to get out of AP Government that day! I knew that I could be doing other things with my time making real money and doing something where I felt appreciated.

But pursuing a soccer career was my dream. More than that, I knew that season with the team was more about who I was becoming than what I was achieving. And after reading Carol Dweck's Mindset, I knew that training the Growth Mindset was one of the most important pieces.
So I recited one of my favorite quotes, "Jamie, do the best you can with what you have right where you are." As the match resumed, I looked around me and saw some cones and a ball. So I set up a ball work drill that I know some of the top class teams in the world do almost everyday. I did that for about 15 minutes.

When I finished, I went over to the guy who handled the team fitness and said, "These guys are out there getting fit right now. What can I do to increase my fitness?" Now, when you ask someone who handles fitness what you can do to grow, they are going to tell you one thing: RUN!!!

So I did an interval workout running around the field while the match was going on. I must have run by the guys coaching at least six times. Not once was there a "Great job Jamie!" or even a glance. That interval run was excruciatingly painful, but I knew it was in my best interest.

When I finished, I knew that I still had an opportunity to learn and grow. So I thought if Brian had as much promise as everyone thought, then there was something to learn off of him. Sure enough, by studying him for the next ten minutes I realized he did one thing very very well. He was constantly looking over his shoulders, taking pictures of the field before the ball came to him. And that little piece was pivotal for me the rest of my playing career.

It wasn't sexy.
It wasn't pretty.
It wasn't easy.
It wasn't acknowledged by anyone else.

But it was that moment where I felt like I had hit rock bottom. It felt like I was the least of all on the team. And it was that moment where I really started letting go of what others were thinking about me, and focused on growth.

Up until that point in my life, I tended to crumble when faced with challenges. If things were hard and weren't in my favor, I would retreat, make excuses, or quit. Having someone younger than me excel was one of the most hurtful things growing up. Not being acknowledged by people who were coaching me was a foreign concept.

But that day was one of the key moments in changing who I was becoming and the trajectory of my life.

I wonder what would happen if in one area of your life you started to embrace challenges, obstacles and setbacks as opportunities to learn and grow? How could things change if in the face of a setback you didn't point the finger but chose to do the best you can with what you have where you are?

Do you feel like you care a great deal about what others think of you? If so, embrace failure. Be willing to look foolish. Stand out for the right reasons instead of fitting in for the wrong ones.

The moment-by-moment choice to have a growth mindset will be one of the hardest things you ever do. And guess what, the training never stops! And remember, **you have to have a growth mindset about having a growth mindset!**

TRAIN To Be Clutch

- In what areas of your life do you feel like you fit in because you are afraid to fail?
- In what areas of your life do you feel the intense pull to prove yourself?
- What are some small things you can begin to do use those contexts as opportunities to learn and grow? Sometimes it's as simple as saying that you need help!

Don't Believe The Myth

Study history.
Study success.
Study greatness.

Rarely is there a pot of gold at the end of your goal. At best it's bronze and at worst it's gravel.

Why do you think so many people with money, power, and fame end up in rehab, broke, divorced, and miserable?

Don't believe the myth.

True satisfaction and fulfillment are not on the other side of achievement. Think about it.... If achievement hasn't filled that void to date, how is more achievement going to fill it in the future?

Make sure you are chasing the things that are truly important. The things you will care about on your death bed.

"You never see a hearse pulling a U-Haul"
-Denzel Washington

Will It Even Be A Blip On The Radar?

Growing up my friends called me a "drama queen," and they were right. I found a way to turn insignificant events into material worthy of the Oxygen Network. Today, my philosophy has changed. When I consult for businesses and top performers all over the world, they often tell me, "It's amazing how simple you can make things." Some of my best friends in LA wonder why I don't let much get to me.

This transformation happened when I started asking myself this simple question: **In five years, will this even matter?** Think about it for a second. Do you remember the angst and worry that you had before your ACT, SAT, or GRE? Do you remember the levels of anxiety you had before your high school basketball tryout? Do you remember how uptight you were before a big presentation with a potential client? How significant are those events now that you are on this side of them?

It doesn't matter what it is, it could be something someone did to you, or it could be a huge contract to do what you love on the biggest stage. The test is the same, and often the answer falls into one of two categories.

1.) You most likely will never remember it happening five years from now.

How do you proceed if this is the case?

- Take some deep breaths
- Let it go
- Write it down on a piece of paper, and flush it down the toilet
- Setup healthy boundaries so similar things do not happen in the future
- Move on to something that really does matter. For example, write a thank you note to one of your friends telling them how much you treasure their friendship.

2.) It could have a massive impact on you five years from now.

How do you proceed if this is the case?

- Control what is in your control
- Let go of the results
- Believe it is in your best interest and an opportunity to learn and grow
- Ask yourself, "What is one thing I can do to make it better?"

The more we worry about something, the more likely we are to experience what we are worrying about. The best thing you can do is let go of the results, have a great attitude, and do your very best. If you do this, the results will probably be what they should be. They may not necessarily be what you want them to be, but they probably will be what they should be. If it won't matter five years from now, don't let it get in the way of having an incredible day today!

TRAIN To Be Clutch

- List out five moments or event that you can remember being extremely anxious about.
- Looking back now, how significant were they?

This Activity Transforms More Lives Than ANYTHING Else

If you really want to get ahead in the world, NEVER READ. I saw a stat the other day that 46% of college graduates never read another book. Incredible! My heroes! If you want to maximize your potential, then stay far away from the wisdom people have garnered through lifetimes of experiences and study. The best thing to do is just watch "Charlie Bit My Finger" on YouTube, and pretend our love of consuming all the wrong things is going to get our country out of over 16 trillion dollars in debt.

We are all guilty of it at times.

It is so much easier to consume than create.
It is so much easier to watch than to read.
It is so much easier to spend than to save.
It is so much easier to build a fantasy football team than to build up a youth football team and equip them with a foundation of excellent life skills.

I believe reading is one of the most underrated activities in the world.

Let me state something at the outset, *I'm not talking about school reading.*

I'm talking about studying autobiographies and other books with wisdom that will not only change your life, but will impact the lives of multitudes around you. Reading is a form of mentorship where we can learn from the greats even if we can't spend personal time with them.

I've literally tricked hundreds of thousands of people into believing that I'm brilliant, BECAUSE I READ ALL THE TIME! I got a 22 on my ACT and a 2.19 GPA my first semester in college. But, I'm able to provide value and now mentor people who are some of the best in the world at their craft. How? BECAUSE I READ things they haven't read, I've applied them to my life and then I've shared what I've learned and how they can apply it to their life, team, and business.

My favorite example of how reading can change the entire trajectory of one's life is Ben Carson. Ben came from a family where his mom was illiterate, his dad abandoned them at a young age, and teachers thought he was stupid. He believed he was stupid and there was nothing he could do about it. His mom asked he and his brother if they wanted to be the dumb kids in class. When they said no, their mom cut TV out of their life and had them read for hours every night when they got home. Ben went from being the stupid kid in class to eventually becoming the greatest pediatric neurosurgeon ever. He is the only person to ever successfully separate Siamese twins attached at the head. He is the chief pediatric neurosurgeon at Johns Hopkins Hospital.

If you aren't happy with where you are in life, then START READING MORE!!!! READ, and then read some more, and DON'T EVER STOP. NONE of your traits are fixed, they can all be developed and grow with hard work, better strategies, and persistence.

One of the girls who plays on the UCLA women's basketball team came up to me on a road trip, and said, "You really read ALL THE

TIME." I said, "Yep, ever since I realized my level of influence was linked to how much I read." If Dr. Ben Carson can become the greatest pediatric neurosurgeon ever from a commitment to reading, then I'm sure I can do SOMETHING in the world if I make the same commitment.

I dare you to spend one year committed to reading a book every two weeks and see what happens.

If Dr. Ben Carson can become the greatest pediatric neurosurgeon in the world from a commitment to reading, coming from his background, then what could we do if we CUT FACEBOOK, TV, CHILLING, and all the other time wasters out of our lives?!

I've learned that there is nothing I'm going through that someone else hasn't been through, made it through, and then written about their experience.

We've created a reading challenge for anyone serious about reaching their personal greatness in business, sports, and life. You can download it for free near the bottom of the page at t2bc.com and a paper copy is available at the back of this book.

Here is a testimonial of someone going through the reading challenge, *"I am pleased to say that I feel like a totally different person mentally since I started this program 18 weeks ago. Thank you for this blessing!"*

TRAIN To Be Clutch

- If you carved out thirty minutes every day, you would end up with 182.5 hours over the course of a year. If the average audiobook is eight hours long, then you could read almost 23 books per year by committing to thirty minutes a day.
- The average NFL game takes close to four-hours to watch on tv when really there are only thirty minutes of play from snap to down. That's nearly 3.5 hours of Bud Light

and Viagra commercials. What if you read a book during that time? I did!

- Tips for reading: don't look at the back and check how many pages there are to read. The book is about acquiring wisdom, not completing the book!

What Are You Playing For?

Now, I know all too well the fire that burns inside of you when someone tells you "you're not good enough", or "you'll never make it", or most hurtful of all, they simply ignore you altogether. I've felt that fire my entire life and used the power of others' underestimation as fuel to push me forward.

In high school, some teachers thought I'd never make it to college. But when I heard that, all I could think about was proving them wrong. It got to the point where those closest to me often told people, "PLEASE don't tell him he can't do something, it won't work out well. He will prove you wrong."

However, all that drive and all that fuel came from negativity: the desire to prove negative assumptions wrong, instead of proving positive assumptions right.

There's a big difference, trust me. Here's how I know.

On February 22nd of 2012, I gave the largest keynote of my life. It was an incredibly energizing experience – two years before, I'd dreamt of attending law school at this university, and here I was onstage, speaking to a packed house. Needless to say, it was amazing. The following day, I got a text from one of my mentors. It was very simple, and yet brought tears to my eyes. It said, "I assume you killed it. How did you feel about it?"

Never in my life had success felt so good. It was so much more fulfilling than proving someone wrong. Because at the end of the day proving people wrong still leaves you feeling unfulfilled, and if we are honest with ourselves, a little dirty on the inside.

When Lebron James was interviewed after he won his first championship, he said something along these lines, "Last year I played to prove everyone wrong, this year I just worked as hard as I could, gave it my very best, and knew I could walk away with my head held high". What voice do you think was louder for him? The voice of his critics or the voice of his supporters?

What most of us really want is for those we love and respect to believe in our dreams, our passions, and our success. And when they do, success is that much sweeter. Because at the end of the day, it feels so much better to say, "See! You were RIGHT!" instead of, "See! You were WRONG."

When we are trying to prove something, we are not tapping into our greatest potential, and we are probably hurting ourselves in the process.

If you have real haters, then you have plenty of people who believe in you. Who are you going to listen to?

TRAIN To Be Clutch

- Your value comes from who you are, not what you do.
- Who do you feel the need to prove yourself too? Very often, those we think we need to prove things to really love us for who we are, regardless of what we do.
- Who are your greatest supporters? Let them know how much their love and support means to you.

Chop Wood. Carry Water.

For as long as his family could remember John had been in love with the Samurai culture. When he was only six years old his family had visited many places in Asia and his fascination turned from boyhood love to deep admiration and respect as he moved into his teenage years.

He had been planning it for a long time, and when he finally turned eighteen, he took a one-way trip to an ancient city in Japan to apprentice under the Samurai archers.

After the excitement of the first few months had started to wear off John started to get a frustrated. During the morning and evenings he was expected to chop wood and carry water from the woods back to the village. It was only for four hours during the heat of the day that he was allowed to practice archery. What frustrated him the most was that he was only allowed to shoot at a straw roll that was seven feet away from him.

One day he approached his Sensei and he asked, "Sensei, how long will it take me to become a Samurai archer? I have dreamed my whole life of being one, but it feels like it will take forever."

The Sensei stopped what he was doing and said, "In the West you want everything instantly, but here you must learn to fall in love with the process of becoming great. Now go chop wood, carry water."

John was confused, but he went back to his normal daily activities.

After a year went by John was finally able to have a Skype video call with his family. John was disappointed to share with them that he hadn't moved past shooting at a target only seven feet away from him, and that the rest of his time was spent chopping wood and carrying water.

As John was talking about his daily routine his dad got a big smile on his face. His dad then asked him who his favorite basketball players were growing up. John responded with Kobe Bryant and Michael Jordan. His dad then told him how Phil Jackson had just released a book, "Eleven Rings," and how he was constantly telling his guys about the necessity of "chop wood, carry water" no matter whether you are winning or losing, the point was to neither get too high or too low, but to focus on the process.

After the call John's spirits were much better.

A few months went by and John was starting to feel very confident with his bow and hitting the seven-foot target. One day while he was practicing his Sensei walked over and John asked him again. How long will it take for me to become a Samurai archer?

His Sensei told him it would take ten years.

John was furious.

"Ten years?! Maybe, if I didn't have to spend so much time chopping wood and carrying water then I would be able to reach my goal much faster!"

The Sensei replied, "If you don't chop wood, carry water, then it will take you 20 years to become Sensei archer." Then he turned and walked away.

John was even more confused and he questioned whether he should quit.

A few weeks went by and John decided he would ask a different Sensei about how long it would take. John made sure he got close to where the Sensei's chopped wood and carried water one morning, and then while they were walking back he asked one of the more friendly Senseis the same question.

This Sensei told him the same thing. John didn't understand, but he then asked, "What if I devote every waking moment to becoming a Samurai archer? No chopping wood, or carrying water, just archery."

The friendly Sensei smiled and said it would take thirty years.

John had reached his emotional breaking point, and he now had tears that started to roll down his cheeks. He blurted out, "but I don't understand!"

The friendly Sensei looked at John with compassion and said, "John the reason it takes longer is because with one eye on the goal, you only have one eye for the journey."

He then went on to tell John stories of people who climb ice mountains, and that if they are focused on the top of the mountain they will not know where exactly where to step next and they will slip and die. The key to ice climbing is to focus on one solid step at a time.

John told the friendly Sensei he understood, and that he would focus on doing his best at archery, chopping wood, carrying water, and letting go of the result.

It was four long and frustrating years before John was able to move up from the seven-foot target to the full targets more than a hundred feet away.

John was very confident when he walked out to the full targets his first day, but his confidence quickly faded as he couldn't even get close to hitting his target.

The bow and arrow started to feel like it was a foreign object in his hands, and he started to once again wonder if all his time had been a waste.

For weeks he couldn't hit the target and his arrows were flaring out all over the place.

Then one day his Sensei went over to check on his progress, and John told him he was thinking about quitting.

The Sensei then told John about the path to mastery, and that he was most likely on a long plateau but eventually he would have another growth spurt.

John was tired of all the philosophical sayings and stories, and he couldn't believe the words that slipped out of his mouth. "You make it sound so easy, but I bet *you* can't even hit the target anymore old man!"

His Sensei calmly responded "Meet me back here at 10 pm tonight."

All day long John was nervous. He knew he shouldn't have spoken to his Sensei in such a disrespectful manner, and he was fearful of what would come next.

Half expecting to get beaten John showed up a few minutes early to scout the scene. At 9:59 his Sensei walked up with his bow and two arrows. John was confused, because it was pitch black outside. You could barely see to walk.

His Sensei walked over to one of the shooting blocks and drew his bow. After a few seconds John watched how his exhale and release were at once intently focused, yet seemingly effortless.

CRACK!

John immediately knew it had hit the target, but it seemed impossible!

Once again, his Sensei picked up his other arrow, and deliberately and methodically drew his bow and then released the arrow.

CRACK!

This time the noise wasn't as loud as the first one, but John was still pretty sure it had hit the target as well. He took off running to the targets, and when he got there he couldn't believe his eyes!

It was impossible! Had he not heard the noises himself, he never would have believed it!

The first arrow was lodged in the middle of the target, and the second arrow had hit the first arrow, splitting it in half, before lodging in the target.

John walked back stunned.

He stuttered, "Hhhhhow did you that? It's impossible!"

His Sensei smiled, and said, "Many years of chop wood, carry water. John, you aim only with your eyes, but I aim with everything. Everything impacts everything. The way I stand, the position of my feet, how much tension I put in the bow, how much tension I have in my hands, how I breathe, and what I see in my mind all impact the end result. Everything impacts everything. Everything is aiming. You have much to learn young John. Get some sleep, and tomorrow we chop wood, carry water."

Stop Planning And Start Preparing

This particular night brought me to tears.

I was on a call with a young woman I get to mentor and I asked her about things that were going on in her life.

She began:
"Well I was planning to graduate early this Christmas and someone in administration messed up my paper work and I found out today that I can't graduate until the following May."

I'm waiting for the outburst of rage....

"But, I guess you just can't plan everything out and now I get to take less hours each semester and spend more time with people and study what I want."

Now if you had heard some of our previous conversations you would know that our work with her may have saved some poor soul's life in the administration office! But what brought me to tears was how when everything around this woman was in chaos, she believed everything was in her best interest and focused her energy and attention on how she could use the situation to her and others' benefit. Not only that, she has learned that there is a difference between planning and preparing.

At best our five and ten year plans are guesses and often don't turn out how we thought they would. There are circumstances that arise that are outside of our control that often make our plans laughable. A slip on the court can render a knee unplayable and will leave a season or career cut short. A downturn in the economy can change the entire trajectory of our retirement plan. A deathly ill family member will cut overseas travel plans short. A sled pops out of the grooves during the start of an Olympic sled race and a medal contending run is over. A beautiful outdoor wedding is crammed inside because of weather conditions. The trip of a lifetime is spent at the airport due to a volcanic eruption thousands of miles away. Whatever it is that we are planning for, there is a good chance that uncontrollable circumstances will disrupt our best-laid plans.

As German Field Marshall Helmuth von Moltke infamously said, "No plan survives first contact with the enemy." But all is not lost!

While our plans are often outside of our control, preparation always lies within. Experience tells me that in any situation we can always learn something. If nothing else, in every context we find ourselves in today we can learn a lot about ourselves, a lot about people, a lot about communication, and a lot about God.

Please, tell me a context in your sport, job, school, leisure, and relationships where those four components are not important. Aside from sleeping I cannot think of one.

A woman who is widely regarded as one of the best physical therapists in the country tells me that people always want to know about how she put her *career* together.
"What?! I don't have a career. I serve people!" She did not have a career, she had a series of challenges.

She tells me that she was almost kicked out of PT school in college and *chose* to work *twice as hard* as her peers only to finish **last** in her class. She went on to do home health for a few years serving people in a very small town. No "at-a-girl's," no accolades. When she moved to another state she opened up a new practice and asked all of the surrounding PT's if they could send her all of the people who they didn't want to work with and all of the people who were not getting better. She wasn't weaving her career together, she was seeking challenges that would refine her to better serve other "souls" as she put it.

She became so excellent in knowing about herself, knowing about people, knowing about communication, and knowing about her discipline that she was eventually asked to serve in one of the most prestigious positions in the country.

She was searching for challenges rather than success.
She was yearning for learning not just validation.
She was trying to become excellent and grow not just someone who was known.

While others were focused on making a living, she was focused on serving and learning.
While others were moaning about difficult patients, she was learning about peoples' tendencies.
While others were writing 5-year plans, she was learning to communicate.

Simply put: While others were planning for the future, she was preparing for the future.

The greatest form of preparing is training. Too many people waste time planning, trying to control the future, which is precious time that could be spent training. They try to plan how the season will go or how the game will flow instead of preparing to handle anything thrown at them. Remember the ceramics study? The group that was graded for quantity, NOT quality, was the group that created the best pots. They learned from doing, not from planning. Preparing is taking advantage of the present moment to prepare you for what is ahead.

My favorite example of this is Jackie Robinson. Most of us have seen the movie *"42,"* which documents Jackie's journey towards becoming the first African-American in Major League Baseball. As is the case with most movies, some of the best parts of the story are left out. If you read Jackie's biography you start to realize that he wasn't the first African-American in the MLB simply because of his ability to play ball. Jackie was given the opportunity because of his character.

Growing up without a father, working multiple odd jobs at a time, doing volunteer work, playing multiple sports, and focusing on his faith in God were all pieces of what made Jackie the best option for Branch Rickey. He was looking for a man of character; someone who had been refined through adversity. He was looking for someone who believed in Jesus's principle of *turn the other cheek*. He was looking for someone who was able to handle abuse, both verbal and perhaps physical, while keeping his head and not retaliating. He was not just looking for skill; he was looking for character.

Character is what Jackie was choosing to train every day of his life, and character is something we either choose to develop or choose to ignore. Everyone wants to play on Jackie's level, but not many are willing to choose to learn from the trials of life. When Jackie was playing at UCLA he had no idea what the future held for him. He couldn't have planned what happened, but his adversity and training had prepared him.

I don't know what situation you are going through right now in school, work, sport or relationships. But I do know this:
Every single thing that has ever happened in your life has prepared you for the present moment. Every context you are in today **_CAN_** *prepare you for something in the future.*

But if we are just playing to win, we're being used by our sport.
If we are just working for money, we're being used by our job.
If we are just working to get a grade, we're being used by education.

But if we are constantly preparing, things change.
You're no longer just doing what the person coaching tells you to do;
you're honing your listening skills and improving your athletic IQ.
You're not just listening to some teacher speak; you're sharpening
your ability to focus when you're bored.
You're no longer earning a paycheck; you're being paid to learn and
grow.

Every moment is **_YOUR_** opportunity!
Stop complaining. Start training.
Burn your goals. Focus on commitments and True Mental Toughness.
Don't just show up. Come ready to grow up.
Don't wait for your turn. Use the opportunity to learn.
Stop planning. Start preparing.

TRAIN To Be Clutch

- What characteristics would you love to adopt? Write out
  at least 3.
- What contexts will you be facing tomorrow that provide the
  training ground for one of those characteristics?

The Best Self-Talk

Tears started to well up in her eyes.

She knew that beating herself up with her self-talk wasn't beneficial, but she didn't know what else to do.

All I asked was, is that how you think Jesus is talking to you when you make a mistake?

That's when the tears started to flow.

From her intake form and from our first conversation I knew that her relationship with Jesus was very important to her, and from my experience I also knew that a lot of people who follow Jesus struggle with negative self-talk more than most.

Somewhere along the line people made her believe that Jesus was mad at her.

I shared a few stories with her about how God actually feels about her, because in the New Testament Jesus said if you have seen me you have seen the Father. Meaning, **how Jesus treated people and cared about the sick, the dying, the diseased, the downtrodden, the outcasts, the screw-ups, the cheats, and the most deplorable members of society is how He feels about you**

171

and me. And He treated all of them with extravagant and relentless unconditional love and grace.

It's not that sin isn't a big deal to God, it is, so much so that He sent His only son to be beaten, tortured, and die a gruesome death on a cross, after living a perfect and blameless life. But through Jesus' death and resurrection our past, present, and future sin has already been taken care of. So all that is left is for us is to trust in Jesus' finished work, and for us to accept the free gift of unconditional love and grace.

Let me explain something I firmly believe. You and I never surprise God. He knew what stupid things I was going to do yesterday, today, and tomorrow. AND He *still* chose to live and die for me, and you, knowing full well all the bad and stupid things we would do.

Denzel Washington put it this way, "I didn't always stick with Him, but He always stuck with me."

There is nothing you or I can do to make God love us more, and there is also nothing you or I can do to make Him love us less. He is talking to you based off of who He is, not based off of what you do, how you feel about Him, or whether you even believe in Him.

So, if that is the case, then are you talking to yourself the way Jesus is after that mistake, that failure, or that setback? Because I can promise His voice is one of encouragement, belief, courage, strength, and unconditional love.

The Resources Myth

Everyday you hear one of the following:

If I just had better people on my team....then
If we just had a better leader....then
If we just had VC money....then
If I just had a better boss.....then
If I worked for that company....then
If I just had the money.....then
If we just had better resources...then

Our perspective is off, and most of the time it's WAY off.

Do you realize there are people all over the world, and possibly right down the street from you, who are literally praying for the resources and opportunities we waste every single day?

Take some time to study people who are world class at their craft and you'll realize most of them built their program, business, or game without world class resources.

John Wooden's teams played in the equivalent of a barn, and for many years never had a true home game because their barn wasn't suitable to host games.

Apple started in a garage. They now have more money than the U.S. government.

Anson Dorrance was still officing out of a shed complete with a portable heater AFTER he'd won 15 national championships.

I created the first mental training apps in the world while living with my mom in a small space between my bed and my brother's bed. Those apps are now in over 56 countries and are transforming the way people train.

Where the first mental training apps in the world were created.

The "lack-of-resources" myth not only cripples creative thinking, but it also has another harmful effect. It limits the people you will attract. People who have achieved certain measures of success perk up when they see and hear about people being resourceful and persevering.

Everyone has brilliant ideas and big dreams, but very few people are willing to take action, be resourceful, and persist in the face of adversity. So, when successful people hear about someone who is doing what they did to become successful, many times they want to help.

Rather than fall into the trap of the resources myth, try and always ask these 2 questions:

What is the smallest version of my dream I can start right now, using what I have, right where I am at?

What is one thing I can do to make this better?

Those who are faithful with little will be trusted with so much more.

Create. Be Resourceful. Persist.

Resources have a habit of following:

Passion
Persistence
Patience

I've learned that everyone has brilliant ideas, but VERY few are willing to sacrifice, work, and persist to transform those ideas to practical and viable solutions.

> *Be faithful in the small things for it is*
> *in them that your strength lies.*
> –Mother Theresa

TRAIN To Be Clutch

- Looking back 2-10 years ago, what do you wish you would have had? How can you create that tool or provide that service for others?
- Wisdom is the most valuable, and most overlooked, commodity in the world. Con you share your wisdom with others? Write out ten things you have learned in life and share it with someone younger.

Your Assumptions Will Kill You

I showed up early, as I was accustomed to doing. It had been almost four months training with this professional team without having a contract. In four months I had received three constructive compliments.

One was from a guy coaching who said, "Jamie, it looks like things are improving." Another was from another guy coaching who said, "Jamie, you are getting stronger." The last was a guy on the team who gave me a fist bump and just said, "Swag!" and I had to count that!

My locker had been moved a few times during those four months due to new players coming in. While everyone else had a printed name-plate above their locker, my name was simply written with a dry-erase marker.

So as I walked in that morning I glanced up at my locker and realized that half my name had been erased. Instead of "GILBERT" all that was up there was "GILB."

Immediately my mind ran towards, "Jamie, they don't want you here. They think you are a great guy but just don't want to say it to

176

your face. They probably erased half your name to ease you out."
The next though was "Oh that was probably _____ letting you
know that because you did not connect the pass to him he wants
you gone!"

Sound familiar?

As I walked across the room to my locker I knew that I had to start
talking to myself. If I just listened, my mind was going to be filled
with nonsense that was not going to be beneficial.

So I started reciting some of my favorite quotes:

Jamie, success comes from doing the best you can with what you
have where you are.

Anything that happens today is in your best interest. It's an
opportunity to learn and grow.

God wants to get you where He wants you to go more than you want
to get where He wants you to go.

On the other side of your greatest fears are some of life's greatest
opportunities.

As the destructive thoughts got louder and louder, I began to listen
to an audio recording that I made of some of my favorite quotes
from my favorite books. Once I was dressed, I headed out to the
field to work on some things before training.

Practice ended up being great and I learned a lot that day. But
because I was also working at my local golf course picking balls off
the range, I had to leave ten minutes early.

So I ran back into the locker room and there was a guy who was
injured standing on my locker. The television was above my locker
and they had lost the remote. So when he finished changing the

channel, he jumped down, and two more letters from my name were missing: "GI."

It had nothing to do with the conclusions that I jumped to in my mind! No one was trying to tell me anything!

Just because we think something, does not mean that it is true. Just because someone says something, that does not mean that statement is the definitive truth. But if we listen to the thoughts in our mind and assume them as truth, most of the time we will come out defeated!

We have anywhere between 30,000 and 70,000 thoughts that come through our mind in a day. Most of those thoughts are limiting beliefs about what is possible, who we are, who God is, and how the world works. People ask me all the time where these thoughts come from and I strongly believe that if the Bible is true in saying that Satan is the father of all lies (John 8:44) and if he really is roaming the earth like a roaring lion waiting for someone to devour (1 Peter 5:8) then it is very likely that many of those thoughts come from Satan.

Regardless of where they come from, you need to know this: **your self-talk is not the thoughts that run through your head; it is what you intentionally say to yourself.**

While we cannot control the thoughts that pass through our minds, we can control which thoughts we accept and how we talk to ourselves. If we are not careful, our assumptions will certainly create the strongholds that will stifle growth and kill us in the process.

One of the most important pieces in becoming who we were created to be is growing in the ability to talk to ourselves instead of just listening.

TRAIN To Be Clutch

- What are you wondering about right now? What school you will go to? Will you get a promotion? Will you have enough money? Why did she raise her eyebrows when she walked by me today? Why didn't he pass the ball?
- What conclusions have you already drawn about others, their motives, or how things will turn out?
- Have you ever been wrong in the past?
- Is that the most beneficial thing to assume?
- What are three controllable things you can shift your mind towards instead?

Lessons From A Kid Who Can't Walk, Talk, Or Feed Himself

Luke is 14 years old and he is one of the happiest people around. Yet he can't walk, talk, or feed himself.

Luke has taught us some extremely valuable lessons in life:

Lesson 1- Use what you have

So many times we get caught up and focus on all the things we don't have in life, and in doing so we make ourselves miserable. The sad part is it doesn't matter how much or how little we have, because there will always be someone who seems to have more than us. As the philosopher Chris Brown said, "The grass is greener where you water it." Luke lives by this philosophy and he definitely makes the most of what he has and is able to do. He loves to try and dunk a small ball in his little tikes goal. He loves for you to get down on his level and wrestle with him. He loves to play catch, and by catch I mean, get hit with the ball, and then throw it nowhere near you! He can't talk, but he can growl and point. And while he sometimes get's frustrated with us for not understanding him, usually he just keeps growling until you get the point. Which brings me to the second lesson.

Lesson 2- Persist no matter what obstacles you face

Luke is the most persistent person I know. He will literally growl, point, and even yell until he gets your attention to do what he wants. If you tell him no, or that you're busy, he just keeps on growling and pointing, until eventually you relent. I often wonder how different my life would be if I showed the same level of persistence in pursuing the things I am passionate about.

Lesson 3- Laugh when you mess up

Luke loves when people fall over, get tackled, or when someone drops something, he belly laughs so hard, you can't help but laugh along with him. He laughs at mistakes. When he misses a dunk, he doesn't care. He just wants to do it again. He loves the act of trying and relishes every moment regardless of the outcome. Sometimes I have a tendency to take things way too seriously, when I need to take a play from Luke's playbook and just laugh at the mistake and try again.

An interesting side note: We tend to get frustrated when people forget something we have taught them, or if we or they make a mistake on things already learned. But do we do this with little kids learning to walk? NO! We would never tell them how stupid they are for falling down and that we already taught them how to walk last week. We encourage them, and we usually do it with a smile. I wonder what would happen if we used that same approach with ourselves and the people we teach, coach, and mentor as we get older?!

Lesson 4- Love unconditionally and SMILE more

One of my favorite things when I get home from a trip is coming home to Luke! He is like a dog in that he loves unconditionally, and when you get home he acts like it is the biggest deal in the world! He often squeals like a little pig, throws his arms out wide, and has the biggest smile on his face, and he desperately wants to give you a hug. Almost everyone who has ever met Luke falls in love with him. His capacity for love comes deep within his heart, and it flows out on everyone he's around.

As I write this, I have tears welling up in my eyes. Here is a kid who can't do so many things we take for granted every day, yet he is able to have an immeasurable impact on the world from a wheelchair. I think he enjoys the few things he is able to do in life more than we enjoy everything we get to do.

My brother Luke inspires me and teaches me things almost everyday, and I hope his story encourages and inspires you as well!

Steal Like An Artist

The pathway to freedom involves stealing. It's that simple.

I'm not talking about taking someone's possessions. I'm talking about studying what they do, and attempting to replicate how they do it until you become a unique representation of how they do things.

Sadly, what happens for most of us, is we compare. We all know what we look like at 4 AM. It's usually not a pretty site. And if you are married, then you know that the bonds of love have to be really really strong!

But what happens is we compare our 4 AM self to everyone else's Instagram highlight reel. You know, they take the best of the one hundred photos from an event, then they crop it to cut out all the bad stuff, they throw on a cool filter that makes the scene seem so exclusive, and then they post if for everyone to see.

Joshua works with a guy who is one of the highest sought after people in photography and he told me the other day it can take up to 200 hours of work to get one commercial photograph!

If there is one thing that I have learned, it is this: No one has it altogether!

When I talk with people who are playing at the highest levels on the PGA, NFL, LPGA, and people in C-Level positions, they all come back to me saying that they feel like it's easier for others. They feel like they don't belong and it's only a matter of time before everyone finds out.

It's so easy to believe, or at least paint the picture, that people who execute at the highest level have something special that we weren't born with. No one is born with "it." We are all born with certain things and "it," whatever "it" is, is developed over time through deliberate practice, intense training, repeated failure, and immense sacrifice.

I can still remember the first time that I heard Ray Lamontagne sing. He sounded like a buttery Ray Charles mixed with a little Etta James! It was awesome! And at that time I just assumed he was *talented* and probably popped out the womb singing like that while strumming a guitar! But when you get behind the scenes, you see the real story.

Daniel Coyle writes that Ray worked in a shoe factory until he was in his early twenties and then cut almost everything out of his life to practice music. He would listen to Ray Charles, Etta James, and Ottis Redding and then try to sing their songs the way they did. He did that for two years.

Let's pause and let that sink in. 730 days.

It took him over eight years until he finally developed the sound that is uniquely him. It was not what he was born with. It's what he developed. It's what he stole and made uniquely him.

Or take a guy named Julian Edleman. He was a back up to Wes Welker on the New England Patriots. Welker was operating at the highest level of anyone else playing wide receiver in the NFL and for most people, Edleman was *stuck* sitting the bench. But the obstacle became the way for Edleman.

Instead of getting upset and simply trying harder, Edleman decided to steal like an artist. He became Wes' shadow for the next year. He studied how Wes studied film. He tried to copy the way Wes made recovery runs after a route. He became so intense in his studying that Wes had to ask him to get away at one point. Over the last few years, Edleman has played at the highest level in his position. He wasn't born that way. He stole like an artist.

Stealing does not only go towards skills. This kind of theft is good for characteristics as well. One of the most limiting beliefs is that the characteristics that we have are set in stone. Carol Dweck's research on Mindsets reveals that our characteristics are malleable. If that is true, then we can adopt desired characteristics and train away less desirable ones.

One of Warren Buffett's favorite exercises is having people think about three people they love, and the characteristics they have. From there, we start to be intentional about adopting those characteristics throughout our day.

One example is a guy I'll call Justin who mentioned a friend that always made him feel accepted and valued. This friend seemed to never judge Justin when they got together. Regardless of Justin's behavior and words, his friend showed him unconditional love.

As we started to get behind the scenes, we realized that his friend is very intentional about treating people with unconditional love. He trains this by reading Scripture, writing out who he himself is in God's eyes, he recites a phrase along the lines of "everyone is created in God's own image," and he is prayerful before most engagements with others. This is not something that he was *born with.* It is something that is developed over time training in the dark.

Another guy who coaches wanted to stop being so sarcastic with the people he was coaching. He realized his words cut deep. So when he felt the urge to say something funny and sarcastic, he would feel the edges of the notecard that was in his pocket. On there he had already written that he wanted to speak less as a whole. But he also wrote out some phrases that he thought would be edifying. Is he perfect? NO! Perfection is not the aim. Growth is what we are going for.

So who do you want to become? What do you want to grow in being able to do? Those things are not for the chosen few. They are developed by those who are willing to steal like artists.

But be warned: this is not for the faint of heart. It will require ridiculous work that will go unnoticed for months, years, and possibly decades.

It's simple. It's not easy.

Train To Be Clutch

- Read *Steal Like An Artist* by Austin Kleon
- What are some characteristics that you would like to let go of?
- What are some that you would like to adopt?
- How can you be intentional this week about choosing to train those characteristics in your life?

There Is ALWAYS A Choice

In the movie, The Book of Eli, one of the characters tells Denzel Washington that he doesn't have a choice. Denzel looks at him and says one of my favorite lines,

"There is always a choice!"

We may not always like the choices in front of us, and we may feel like our choices are limited, but there is always a choice. If we are honest with ourselves, most of the time there are almost an unlimited amount of choices. We may not like the most likely consequences of those choices, but there is a choice. The first step to engagement is realizing that we have autonomy.

If we believe someone else is controlling us, then we are most likely going to comply. Compliance sucks. Compliance is going through the motions, and going through the motions never created something of exceptional value.

The other thing about compliance is it tends to shift the responsibility from our shoulders to the controlling party's.

When we realize we have a choice, we are free to engage with those around us, and give everything we have to get better everyday. We understand our attitude and effort play a monumental role in our development and the fruits of our labor.

Make the choice to engage, and don't be a robot!

When I make the choice to not engage, the person I am hurting the most is myself.

Somehow internally signals have gotten crossed and we forget we are hurting ourselves when we don't fully engage. Whether it is in school, work, training, or anything else we miss out on the next level by not becoming the best we can become at this level.

Even if you don't like your leadership team, parents, or your teammates, you still want to give 100% to become the best that you can be at this level, BECAUSE IT WILL PREPARE YOU FOR THE NEXT LEVEL. Are your leaders going to know everything to do in every situation? NO. Are they going to make mistakes? YES, but if you don't ENGAGE, you will not be getting better ever day, AND IT WILL DIMINISH YOUR CHANCES AT THE NEXT LEVEL.

You decide what you are going to do and who you are going to be everyday. Even choosing to do nothing is still making a choice.

THERE IS ALWAYS A CHOICE.

A Specific And Sincere Compliment

Anson Dorrance taught me a very valuable lesson. He taught me that a specific and sincere compliment can change the entire trajectory of a person's life. He doesn't even know he taught me this, but he will after he reads this. He didn't share this lesson with me. *He showed me.*

It probably took him less than a minute to type this email to me, "Joshua, your workshop was EXCELLENT! I loved your story, your content, and your delivery." *It may have not meant a lot to him at the time, but it meant the world to me.*

It has fueled me for the last three years and it has changed not only the trajectory of my life, but the lives of those I have had the privilege of impacting.

We don't need 21 national championship titles to impact someone's life with a specific and sincere compliment. I've had the pleasure of meeting a lot of people around the world, but one of my favorite people by far is Kelia Moniz. She has a presence unlike anyone I have ever met. When she walks into a room everyone can feel her presence. She is one of the sweetest and kindest people around. The first time I met her we were standing outside of Cheesecake

Factory after church and I asked her, "Where does your swagger come from?" She told me it came from God. I was intrigued, and that was pretty much the end of the conversation as we went separate ways.

Our mutual friend, Ryan, told me she won a world championship for surfing. Later that night I sent her a tweet encouraging her and telling her about the impact her presence has on people. I gave her a specific and sincere compliment. I also sent her some tools and told her I would love to sit down with her if she ever had the time.

The next afternoon we sat down at a street side pizza shop in Westwood, California, and I poured into her life. I told her a lot of stories and encouraged her with lots of specific and sincere compliments. On multiple occasions tears welled up in her eyes and I could see her fighting to keep them from flowing down her face.

I was shocked! Here is a girl who has reached the pinnacle of her sport, who is surrounded by some of the most powerful people in the world on a daily basis, yet my words were clearly moving her in powerful ways.

There is power of life and death in our words. Use them wisely.

Sometimes it is the person we would never guess needs it who could benefit the most from a specific and sincere compliment. Oftentimes it is the very thing we think someone knows they bring to the table that we actually need to compliment.
I've personally experienced it, and I've seen the impact on hundreds of people.

Write a note.
Send a text.
Leave a voicemail.

Make sure you don't ever miss an opportunity to give a specific and sincere compliment.

TRAIN To Be Clutch

- In leadership, one of our commitments should be giving specific and sincere compliments to between 2-5 people each day. These are not Dr. Phil sessions!
- What are some of the specific compliments you have received? How have they impacted you?

Looking Back, Many Of The Lions I Chased Were Actually Kitty-Cats

Joshua called me one day and told there was a lady who coached a college program that wanted to do a workshop. The timing didn't work for Joshua, so he encouraged me to call her and see what we could work out.

When I was in middle and high school, I wasn't the best at talking to people on the phone. Anytime I got on the phone with a girl I *dreaded* silence! One way I found to help with the silence was to write out a list of things to talk about before we got on the call so that during any form of silence I could fill the void with what looked like an early version of a drop-down menu on my note pad.

I must admit that getting on the phone with people I didn't know scared me up until my late twenties. So as I prepared for this call, I jotted down some questions that I wanted to ask.

I dialed the number and it went to voicemail. So I left a message saying, "Hi, this is Jamie Gilbert with Train To Be Clutch. Joshua mentioned that you were interested in doing a team workshop but that the timing became an issue."

From there, I am not sure what I said, but I know that I said something that sounded a little funny, and then I paused....

......

......

for what felt like eternity, but what was more likely only four or five seconds!!!

At this point, I smiled and thought to myself, "Alright mental training ninja, are you going to believe that this is in your best interest?"

After about 10 seconds of pause, I thought, "I know there is a number on this keypad that will allow me to rerecord." I just didn't know which one! So, I pushed every button on the keypad!!!! It sounded like jingle bells on the message for sure.

At this point I was probably 60 seconds into the message.

When that didn't work I figured that the message would run out of time and there might be a prompt that would ask me if I wanted to rerecord. Just to cover my bases I got on my macbook and googled "How to erase a voicemail and rerecord." The first response said that 99% of all voice message services will allow you to rerecord if you just press the pound key.

"Maybe I didn't try that one," I thought.

Pound. Nothing happened.

Pound. Nothing happened.

Pound. Nothing happened.

Finally a prompt came up and said "Goodbye!"

I laid down my iPhone, sat back in my chair with a smile, and asked a growth mindset question: "If you could do this all over again, what would you do differently?"

The answer was clear. I would have embraced the pause and been a little bit vulnerable saying, "I'm sorry about that little stumble!"

So I called back and left another message saying that I was sorry about the first one and that if she wanted to call back that I would love to chat with her.

She never called!

I was extremely bummed. I really wanted to share stories with her team and I could have certainly used the finances at the time. But that moment, which felt like rock bottom, (even though I know this was not rock bottom) actually became the springboard for me moving forward. In the subsequent weeks I jumped on the phone with countless people and Joshua actually asked me to talk to people who were interested in working with him!

Why? Well, I can't say I know all of the things that were in play, but having got out of my comfort zone on that call, I felt like no other call could be worse. If that was worst case scenario, then any other call would be a cakewalk.

What I know is that too many of us are fitting in for the wrong reasons, instead of standing out for the right reasons. We are afraid of failing, looking dumb, or being uncomfortable. But when we go to the edges of our comfort zone, we realize that the things that scare us are essential for our growth. And looking back, we usually realize that those little fears are ridiculous! When we thought we were chasing lions, we were really only chasing kitty-cats!

My hunch is that you will look back at your current situation five years from now laughing and shaking your head.

Joshua 1:9 "Have I not commanded you: be bold and very courageous!"

Oh, and if it was your voicemail I left the message on and you are reading this now, I am still up for that call!

TRAIN To Be Clutch

- What are 3 areas in your life where you feel like you are simply playing it safe?
- Like my fear of pause in conversations, what terrifies you?
- In what ways could you step outside of you comfort zone and challenge yourself?
- My guess is that doing so will not result in serious injury, loss of your job, or death. What is the worst-case scenario?
- Read *In A Pit With A Lion On A Snowy Day* by Mark Batterson

The Pursuit of Happiness Is Killing Us

Kevin Durant sat down with Bill Simmons in an interview, and in this interview Durant was asked about the nicknames he had been given. He said he did not like most of them, and he would prefer to be called, "The Servant....I just like to serve everybody, my teammates, the ushers at the game, fans."

It's not every day you hear something like that come out of someone's mouth, but then again, not many people in the world can do what Kevin Durant can do on the basketball court.

I find this most interesting because in a world of "what can you do for me," Kevin Durant seems focused on the exact opposite, "what can I do for others." He seems to be others focused in not only thought, but also deed. Whenever the tornadoes struck the Oklahoma City area, he was one of the first people to make a seven-figure donation to help those affected.

Through conversations with many people around the world it seems rare to find the level of service Kevin Durant is committed to. It seems we have an obsession with happiness. We could call it the pursuit of happiness. Many times when people fill out our intake forms before workshops they answer the question, "What is your big dream?" with "To be happy."

Here is the problem, happiness and fulfillment are oftentimes in direct opposition to one another. *Happiness is more about instant gratification.* It is a feeling that seemingly comes and goes. Someone or something can make you happy for a little while, but that feeling can fade and you'll need something new to make you happy once again.

For some people their pursuit of happiness might come from the purchasing of new clothes, shoes, or cars. For others it might be in having lots of cool friends or the most beautiful significant other.

A prevalent characteristic of happiness talk is a strong degree of selfishness. *Happiness is all about me.* How **I** feel.

Another predominant characteristic of happiness is that it is easy. If I have to work really hard for something and put in a lot of blood, sweet, and tears, then I will be sacrificing a lot of short-term happiness, so that is unacceptable. Happiness is supposed to be easy.

The two predominant characteristics of happiness are that it must come *easy* and it is *me* focused.

Here is the ironic twist. Fulfillment is often in direct opposition to happiness. **Fulfillment is *others-focused* rather than *me-focused*, and it comes through going through the tough stuff.**

When you ask people in the later stages of life what are the most fulfilling things they have done in their life, they often tell you things like climbing mountains and raising children. When you ask them what were the most challenging things they have done in their life, they tell you things like climbing mountains and raising children.

Over the last 100 years our "quality of life" has done nothing but continue to climb higher and higher in the United States, yet during that same time so have the amount of people on antidepressants and those taking their own life.

I'm afraid the pursuit of happiness is killing us.

Fulfillment is a much deeper and abiding feeling than short-lived happiness. I fear many people are missing out on fulfillment in the pursuit of happiness. I think we could all learn from Kevin Durant and seek out opportunities to serve others. If we did so, I think we would experience a lot more fulfillment even though we might sacrifice some happiness.

TRAIN To Be Clutch

- The **BIG LIE** is that satisfaction and fulfillment are found somewhere higher on the ladder. Happiness and fulfillment are often in direct opposition to each other. By seeking and pursuing one, we will most likely miss out on the other.
- Happiness is most often me-focused and comes through the easy road.
- Fulfillment is most often others-focused and comes through the tough challenges.
- Fulfillment is a much deeper and abiding feeling than short-lived happiness. If you want fulfillment, you most likely have to sacrifice short-term happiness.
- What are some opportunities you have in your life right now where you could shift from "what can I get?" to "how can I serve?"
- Who do you know that is a willing servant? What is it like to be around that person?
- What are some things the pursuit of happiness has cost you?

Clamoring Around the Mirror....Really?

I'll never forget the dreary, wet, and miserable days when we were sitting in the dressing room in Ireland ready to play a football (soccer) match. I treasure those memories! One of the funniest things to me was that even though the upcoming game was huge, the most important thing was the shape of everyone's hair. Seriously, you've never seen so many grown men exerting so much effort as they clamored for their moment to make sure the comb over was perfect and the eyebrows were straight.

"If we put that kind of attention to detail into our training and preparation, maybe we'd have won the league!"

Here is the simple principle:

We are intentional about what we value.

I have the opportunity to speak with people from all walks of life about their dreams and passions and I tend to hear very similar things:

I want this.
This is what I want to do.

This is what I want to accomplish in my career.
This is where I want to go.
This is who I want to become.

Now it's our belief the only statement we have control over is the last one: who you become.

And by the time I can convince people the only controllable is who they are becoming, I hit them with a question:

"What did you set out to deliberately do today to become that person?"

Silence....

You see it's great to have an idea of the type of person we want to become, but if we are not intentional about how we will grow towards that today, then I think we're just throwing out little more than a *hope or a wish*. I've talked to countless people who say they hope to play professionally, but how they use their time and the strategies they've compiled are almost laughable. I can hear Deon Sanders loud and clear, "Come On Man!!!!"

When most people reach out to me it's usually because they want to get the edge by tackling the mental game. Great.

"Let's plan on working together every week for the next 3 months," I tell them. They say, "What?"

You see, a lot of us are out for the quick fix. People in coaching often complain the people on their team want a quick fix. However, the people coaching often want the quick fix as well, and they show the same frustration as the people on their team in many different scenarios in front of their team.

We like the food to be delivered fast and we don't want to wait for better food. We want the hour and half movie instead of the

12-hour book, and we want to be the best in the country but we don't want the minimum 10,000+ hours of pain, struggle and deliberate practice to get there. No, no, no, no, no! There is a progression. There is a route. It's called *the path to mastery*!

There is a word that often goes overlooked and unnoticed: Train. I tell people all the time our brand is not *"think to be clutch," "get some knowledge and you will be clutch," "hope to be clutch," "transfer to be clutch," "wait on your moment to be clutch"* or *"do this once and be clutch,"* it's **TRAIN** To Be CLUTCH.

By train I am talking about ***deliberate, consistent and intentional*** training of your mind, heart and body.

It's not waking up and saying you want to be great at your sport. It's waking up saying how you are going to be intentional about getting better today.

It's not sitting down to just watch a game. It's strapping in for 2 hours of film study and purposeful visualization.

It's not just showing up to practice ready to jump when told. It's arriving early and going over your highlight reel, writing down 2 ways you will get better regardless of what happens in practice and writing out 2 people who will make sure have a great day.

It's not breaking it down with the team and showering up. It's breaking it down, taking game shots from game spots at game speed, and writing out 15 specific things that went well, 2 areas for growth, 2 things you learned and the vision for your life.

That is training.

It's deliberate.
It's consistent.
It's intentional.

It's life changing.

Check Yourself

If you want to play point guard exceptionally well, spend less time posting selfies in your new snap-back on Twitter and start using that phone to video your movements so you can *study* how to be quicker and more agile.

If you want to excel in school, stop watching television and criticizing all the people on *The Voice* who are pursuing their dreams and *start reading and learning* from people who know and have done more than you have.

If you want to play at an elite level athletically, stop telling yourself and others what you want to achieve and start doing the things to close the gap between where you are and where you want to be. **Study those who were great at what they did: Michael Jordan, Tiger Woods, Kevin Durant, Lebron James, Jerry Rice. You'll find that they were the first in, last out.**

If you really care about who you are becoming and if you really care about stretching towards your dreams, then don't come into the locker room and complain about having to do the same drills over and over. Don't sit down in the leaders' office after a game and talk about someone else's mistakes. Don't sit down with your friends or by yourself at night and list out all the reasons why other people or outside influences are to blame for your lack of growth. Don't complain to other people in CEO positions about the new generation of workers. Don't complain to other people in coaching about this generation of entitled kids. Do something to make it better!

You need to get real with yourself. You need to honestly document how you spend time for a week and see if that is congruent with the size of your dreams. You need to take an honest look at whether or not you are actually applying resourcefulness in your life. You need to examine your thoughts every night this week and question whether or not they are fixed or growth mindset. And you need to read more!

You see, we don't just become clutch. We *TRAIN* to be clutch. We don't just become great parents. We train to be great parents. We don't just become Godly. We train ourselves in Godliness. We don't just become who we want to be. **We become the person we trained to be.**

Everyday, with every choice, we are training. No matter whether you are nine years old or seventy-five years old; no matter if you are playing pickup or are playing in the NBA, every choice creates a pathway for how we will act in the future. The question is are we building the roads in our muscle memory to take us where we want to go? Are we training to become who we want to become?

If you really want to take steps towards training to be mentally tough, start here. We believe our definition of true mental toughness is unrivaled.

True mental toughness is giving your very very best, having a great attitude, treating people really really well, and being unconditionally grateful regardless of your circumstances.

Now that all sounds great, but how many of us actually do this, or know someone who does, everyday? Not many. You see, *it is hard* to have a great attitude in the middle of a season when you're 5-11. *It's extremely difficult* to treat other people well when you've had a horrible previous game and are sitting on the bench. *It's close to impossible* to be grateful when you are sitting out most of your senior year due to an injury. These things don't happen naturally. They aren't comfortable and they aren't our default mode of operation. But they can be if you are willing to be intentional and deliberate in actions.

Here's what you do. Today, never mind tomorrow because tomorrow will soon be today, write out each component of mental toughness and before it write, "Today I choose." Then write out how you will specifically apply this today.

Now here is the key. You need to write out *specifically* how this will play out in your daily activities. Most of us have a pretty good idea of the context we will be in and the people we will be around in our day. Though we don't know all of the specifics, we can work with what we think will happen. So here is how mine worked one day:

Today, I choose to give maximum effort when I write. Even though I know I will hit roadblocks and want to search things on the internet, I will fully engage in my writing for the 2 hours I have allotted.

Today, I choose to have a great attitude when my wife asks for help with our sick 18 month old. Even though I have plenty of calls to make, I will gladly serve her and my son sacrificially.

Today, I choose to treat _____ better than *I think* this person deserves. Even though they have treated me poorly I choose to love them as Christ loves them.

Today, I choose to be grateful that I can walk, talk, see, and hear. Even though I am not who I want to be or where I ultimately want to be, I am so grateful for the blessings God has bestowed.

Today, I choose to practice these things regardless of my circumstances.

This is such a *simple* thing to do that it will probably go overlooked by most. It may not have a great effect on you today. 3 weeks later it may not seem to be super effective. But if we are serious about the type of person that we want to become, 3 months, 6 months, and even a year from now we will know this practice is changing our life.

Be deliberate.
Be consistent.
Be specific.
Be the change that you want to see in the world.

But know this, until your intentionality in becoming the person you want to be scratches your intentionality in what you eat, until it matches your intentionality in how you make money, and until it exceeds your intentionality in how you dress and present yourself, your growth in becoming that person will continue to simply be a wish.

Living With Intentionality

I had the pleasure of reading the book *Toughness* by Jay Bilas a few summers back and of the many things I took away, nothing stood out more than this:

"If I could go back and be a player again, one area in which I would strive to be better would be my daily preparation. I would take more time to mentally prepare myself for practice. It would have made me a far better player if I had consistently taken the extra time to mentally prepare myself and focus on what I expected to get out of that day's practice, and to mentally prepare myself to truly compete that day, from the first drill to the last."

After reading that I decided to commit to beginning every practice, every training session, and every game by sitting in my father-in-law's green Dodge Stealth with a pen and notecard in hand. I decided to write out two specific areas I was going to get better in regardless of what the people coaching had us do, and I was going to make 1-2 peoples' days great. Since putting this to practice, my life, my game, and my influence have been radically different.

Specific Areas of Growth
I remember our team having just come back from a two-game trip only to be playing the next night at home. Sitting in the parking lot in the green Dodge Stealth I wrote out that I was going to work on

my vision (ability to see my surroundings instead of looking at the ball), and my resolve to sprint when we were in transition from offense to defense and vice versa.

As we were about to start into our team warm-up the guy coaching us said that the guys who played in both games were only going to do 30 minutes of the warm-up and then rest while the others played for 45 minutes. Immediately you could tell what the majority of us who played the games were thinking: "Coach said I don't *have to* train today." I know this because almost all of the guys went through the warm-up laughing and talking about the weekend, and a few didn't even tie their boots!

Here's what I know: the warm-ups we do in soccer in the states are what many top professional clubs around the world do as their actual practice. They are just focused and do it at a higher level. So I know that the "warm-up" is actually a world class training ground and because I was equipped with two ways to get better, my half-hour of training was deliberate.

After the "warm-up" we sat off to the sidelines and watched as the rest of the team played a match. I know he said I had to sit, but he didn't say I couldn't *train*. I decided to work on my vision for 15 minutes by watching a specific person and looking for patterns of movement on offense. Then I imagined that I was on the red team and visualized myself making transition runs into dangerous areas. Knowing that our brains can't tell the difference between what is perceived and what is real, I made sure to play even though I wasn't physically playing that day.

Make Someone's Day Great
One day before practice I was sitting in my father-in-law's green Dodge Stealth and I wrote down on an index card that I was going to make someone's day great. I didn't know who or how, but I was going to focus on doing it.

There was a guy who turned up at training who no one had met before and I could tell by his body language that there might be a struggle that day. I know what it's like to be the new guy on the team. We are usually quiet and we play small. And that is exactly what happened. The young man, call him John, didn't play at a very high level that day, but I saw two flashes of play where I could see some untouched potential.

At the end of training John was sitting off to the side of the team taking off his boots, and I reminded myself that I was going to make someone's day great. So I got up and walked over to him in front of the whole team, stuck out my hand, and said, "Hi my name is Jamie." You could hear a pin drop! He introduced himself and told me where he was from where he played in college. Very quickly I said to him, "Hey man, I know things weren't great today for you, but I want to let you know that I saw two things that tell me you can play at a very high level." I continued to share with him the specific instances I remembered and he started to smile. We continued talking for 30 minutes and then went our separate ways.

John continued to show up for training and his transformation was quite remarkable. He went from not being on the team, to being in the second team. From being on the second team, to scoring goals against the first team. From scoring goals against the first team to playing in the first team. And from being in the first team to playing a pivotal role at the end of the season. The best part of it all, was that he called me a few months later with some of the most moving words I've ever heard:

"Jamie, I want to thank you for sharing everything you did with me this summer. I don't know if you know this, but that night you introduced yourself to me, I was about to drive home and pack it in. I wasn't going to come back. It was clear that I couldn't play at this level, and really I wasn't sure if I was going to keep playing soccer. But your words really struck me and caused me to stick it out. I'm going into this season with a renewed confidence and clear thought as to how I will improve. I feel like I've changed and even my family says I am a different person. So thank you!"

Wow! Now I don't tell that story to make myself sound like a saint. But where did all of that start? Most people say it stemmed from sticking my hand out an introducing myself. But that's not it. I sat in the car before practice and *wrote down* that I was going to make someone's day great.

For all of the things that we teach on *you* as the individual, we hope our heart comes across clear that true fulfillment and true purpose involves our relationships with others. When we become intentional about what be believe, how we think, and what we do, we become the types of people who can start tidal waves of influence around the world.

TRAIN To Be Clutch

- Before you get to work, before you go to school, before you go to practice or a game, and before you start making breakfast for your kids sit down and write these two things out:
1. Two ways in which I will improve today
2. One person whose day I will make great

Keep Reading

I'll admit it; I want to know what is going to happen in the next 365 days. I want to know where my family will be living, what we will be focusing on, how much money we will have, and what kind of opportunities will arise from there. Like Violet in Willy Wonka and the Chocolate Factory stomping my feet madly I am thinking, "I want it NOW!"

I was going through this mad stomping in my prayers one day when a thought came to my mind from the past: "Jamie, keep reading."

While I was in Bible college I had a teacher that would have us open the Bible and start reading. Anytime we had a question, his default response would be, "Keep reading."

I can't tell you how frustrating that was to hear this phrase over and over again. But it was interesting that many times when we kept reading we would stumble upon the answer to our question.

Sometimes, however, the answer wouldn't appear. When we asked about that, he made a great point, "Maybe your question was the wrong question."

Maybe your question will never be answered and the things that you want now will be inconsequential in the near future. But it was interesting that when I was recently hit with that wisdom from the past, that in the next week my question was answered. Since then it has become a mantra in my life. When I want things to happen RIGHT NOW, I hear that beautiful phrase, "Jamie, keep reading."

It reminds me of a quote from Steve Jobs: "You cannot connect the dots looking forward, but you can always connect them looking back."

One of the reasons we talk about burning goals is that we find so many people who have achieved what they set out to reach only to find that it was unfulfilling and that they weren't actually passionate about what they do. In their climb towards that pinnacle they have sacrificed relationships, their own health, and often their own integrity in the process of what they *thought* they wanted.

Others have not hit each step that they put down in their five-year plan and grow insanely frustrated with where and who they have become.

We will continue to say it again and again, **the only thing that matters is who you become and the effect you have on others in the process.**

When people ask me how I started my speaking career I always tell them about hustling kiwis and cucumbers in outdoor fruit markets in Ireland. My goal was not to have a consulting firm and write books. But focusing on my ability to communicate and connect with other people afforded me the opportunity to step in as a mentor for a non-profit in Dublin. From there I had the opportunity to answer phones at an insurance agency. From there I had the opportunity to clean peoples' golf clubs at my local course. From there I had the opportunity to train a nine year old in soccer. And from there things have grown into the capacity I have to serve with Train To Be Clutch.

If you are frustrated about where you are, my advice to you is to keep reading. By that I mean keep learning, keep beating on your craft, keep listening to people who know more than you, keep experimenting, keep training even when you don't feel like it, and literally keep reading.

Stop waiting for your moment and keep training for your moment so that when the opportunity of your dreams comes, you won't flinch, you won't fret, but you'll step up and trust your training.

TRAIN To Be Clutch

- Looking back, are there any questions or anxieties that you had that were resolved in due time?
- What are you anxious about right now? What can controllable things can you do to shift your energy in a more beneficial direction?

One Of The Worst Evils Around

Once upon a time an old evil witch was going out of business and she had a yard sale to sell her powers and tools.

All of her usual tools were out for sale, and had been cleaned and polished for display. You could buy all the traditional tools you think of when you think of evil: jealousy, anger, lust, pride, envy, deceit, and adultery. Droves of people flocked to the sale and all her tools were sold to the highest bidder.

Towards the end of the day, after all the tools had been well picked through, all that was left were a few trash heaps of old worn-out and broken tools. One gentleman dug through the scraps and found a tool that was very well worn, and looked like it was on its last leg. He brought it to the woman to ask how much.

The old evil witch replied, "That tool is too valuable for me to sell, it is the only one I'm passing down to my niece. Give it back to me. It should not have been out here!"

Now the man was even more intrigued. "But it is so worn, and yet you claim it is worth more than all these other shinier and newer tools. I must know what this tool is."

The witch pried it from his hands and asked him to leave. She took the old tool back and hid it in her house.

Eventually the day came to an end and all the tools and scraps had sold, except the one the witch had hidden.

A few months later the witch was on her deathbed when she called for her niece to come visit. Her niece was very angry she had sold all her fancy tools.

"How could you sell all your tools and not pass them onto me?!" She shouted.

The old witch waited for her to calm down and she then she told her to look under her bed. The niece looked under the bed but all she saw was an old, worn-out tool.

"This?! This old thing is all you left me?!"

The old witch looked at her and said, "Oh how naive you are young child. This tool is discouragement, and it is more powerful than all the other tools combined. The best part is that most people never suspect that it comes from you. Discouragement will allow you to get to a person's heart when none of the other tools will, and once they become discouraged they are putty in your hands. You can squash dreams, level the greatest of ideas, and ruin almost anything in the world without detection all by using this tool to plant the seeds of discouragement."

Eventually the niece realized the power of discouragement and even though it was her only tool, she went on to become the most powerful witch in all the land.

TRAIN To Be Clutch

- In what ways has discouragement from others hampered your life?

- Do you use discouragement and shame to get others to perform?
- Instead of shame, how can you encourage and cast vision for those you lead and serve?

This Is Who I Am

Imagine how laughable it would be if an adult was crawling around on all fours telling people, "I don't need to learn how to walk, this is who I am."

Now picture my face when someone coaching or playing tells me something very similar, "I'm a _____, this is who I am." MEANING, "I can't or won't put in the effort to change." Most of the time it is something like, "I'm a screamer," "I'm not a reader," or some other excuse for not learning and growing.

Will it be easy? Never.

Will it be extremely time consuming? Yes.

Is it past possible? YES.

John Wooden is widely considered the greatest person in coaching of all time with 10 National Championships, a winning percentage of 80%, and United States presidents who called him one of the biggest influences in their lives. **Yet, even the 'Wizard of Westwood' was constantly tweaking what he did and trying to learn and grow.** Later in his career it got more honed in, but even he was still learning, growing, and he highly encouraged those traits in those around him. I've talked to people who saw Wooden sitting on the front row of lectures in his nineties with pen and paper taking notes. Of all people, it would have been easy for him to say, "Do you not know who I am?! I should be the one giving the lecture." But he was the consummate learner, always trying to get a little bit better.

Anson Dorrance is another one of the greatest people in coaching, yet he took notes for 2 hours during my workshop. He reads more than almost anyone I know. He is always trying to learn and grow.

Jay Z grew up in the Marcy Housing Projects in Brooklyn, and he sold drugs as a way of providing for himself. If Jay Z never changed strategies he would most likely be in prison today. He had to shift gears and change strategies in order to get to the next level. If he didn't stop engaging in illegal activities he wouldn't be able to be an entrepreneur whose net worth is over half a billion dollars. Selling drugs might have gotten Jay Z out of the projects, a lot of street cred, a couple nice whips, and a lot of J's, but he had to change strategies in order for him to become who he wanted to become. He changed strategies and slowly became, as he is famously quoted as saying, "I'm a business.....man".

What got you to this level will rarely get you to the next level. If you want to reach your fullest potential, you must constantly be willing to learn, change and grow.

TRAIN To Be Clutch

- List out four of your dominant "I am" statements. Be honest. Are these the most beneficial beliefs?
- If not, what would be more beneficial to believe about yourself?
- What are some characteristics you would love to have? Who models them?

Maybe YOU Are The One Getting In The Way

I received a text from a guy I get to train who plays college golf. He has thousands of hours of training under his belt but was struggling during his second of three rounds in his tournament. Asking for advice, I asked him what was one area he could work on/improve on the next day.

He chose to focus on putting and admitted that the way he putted on the practice green did not match what he did during the round. On the practice green his process was short: place the ball, read the green, stand up and strike it.

When he reached the green during a tournament the length of the process increased: read the green, get the line on the ball in line with his read, practice stokes, and then strike. By his own admission, all of that made him feel very tense.

So I asked him, "If I had you close your eyes while I put the ball on the green and then had you open them with only 10 seconds to putt, how do you think you would do?"

"I think I would do pretty well!" he replied.

I didn't tell him to take only 10 seconds in his process, but I challenged him to think about what he does in his process that may not be necessary. Doing practice swings because that's what everyone else does is NOT a good reason to do them. "Don't speed up," I told him, "but cut out the things you think are unnecessary."

That's not just good golf advice, that's good life advice. Don't just do things because others are doing them. Don't just do it to be different and stand out. Do it because you think there is merit in it and because you want to. Authenticity comes from choosing to operate out of love instead of fear.

Back to my friend and his tournament. The next day he texted me back and said he was -4 with only 23 putts! He had cut his process down to around 10 seconds, again, not speeding up, but cutting out the unnecessary. On top of that, he kept telling himself he was an awesome putter. And lastly, he was reading Adam Braun's *The Promise Of A Pencil* in between holes. Yeah, you can do that!

It's pretty amazing, but let me say that I'm not too surprised. What my friend was actively involved in was shutting down the over-analytical side of his brain, and letting his muscle memory begin to take over.

In her book *Choke,* Dr. Sian Beilock reveals her research conducted with people in high-level golf.

"In my Human Performance Laboratory, we have shown that skilled golfers putt better when we instruct them to putt as quickly as possible. Of course, new golfers need plenty of time to think about what they want to do, because attending to the step-by-step details is important when you are just learning the tools of your trade. But once a skill is well practiced, too much time—allowing for too much attention to detail—can be a bad thing."

Again, *quick* does not mean rushed. It simply means not dwelling.

For all intensive purposes, she dumbs it down to, this:

The right side of our brain is analytical; the left side houses the creativity and memory. We want to occupy the right side and let the left side come out. It's kind of like trying to occupy the overpowering Uncle at a family gathering so that others can enjoy their time. (You might think that sounds horrible, but don't act like you haven't been there) Beilock goes on to say:

"Having a golfer count backwards by threes, for example, or having a golfer sing a song to himself uses up working-memory that might otherwise fuel overthinking and a flubbed performance."

It really comes down to this: we have to talk to ourselves instead of just listening to ourselves. We need to get in our own way, but in the right manner. There needs to be a reason behind what we say. But we don't need to analyze every single detail. Like Ray Allen catching a pass in the corner, we need to spot up, catch, and release fluidly as though we have done this thousands of times.

And this is what my man did. He shortened his process and did what was unique and good for him. He let go of anxiety and occupied his right side of the brain to let the left come out. And by doing all of this he exuded trust in the fact that he is very *very* good at putting.

Will everyday yield the same results? Maybe, maybe not. But I have a hard time believing that if he is TRAINING the ability to operate from left-side memory that the results won't lean towards lower numbers more consistently.

Who knows though? There is no guaranteed ROI (return on investment) for anything we do. But we do it in faith. More on that next time!

So those of us who don't play high level golf, what can we take away?

1. Don't do things JUST because others are doing them. That goes from what you wear each day to what you do during your lunch hour at work. That goes from how you interact with your kids to the plan, or lack thereof, that you try to get your golf swing on. What I know is that many of us copy and repeat what we have seen, because we are afraid to step out. But rarely have the people we admire don't what the group would say was socially acceptable. Operate out of love, not fear.

2. Talk to yourself instead of just listening. What science tells us is that we have anywhere between 15,000-60,000 thoughts going through our mind in a day. Equipped with a learned negativity bias, we tend to ruminate on things that aren't most beneficial for us. For some of us, myself and Joshua included, we think much of those thoughts are lies from the Devil. Regardless of where they come from, we have the choice in what we entertain and believe. If we are sowing things that are truthful, helpful, and good, then we will tend to find those things coming out in our lives. If you'd like an audio track that helps you sow beneficial beliefs, email Jamie@traintobeclutch.com for the audio.

Regardless of where you are and regardless of what you do, you have the power to choose what you fix your mind towards. The person, flesh and blood on this earth that has the most to do with you, is you.

Train To Be Clutch

- If it's true that 90% of our thoughts are the same things we thought the day before, then there are some obvious patterns in what we think.
- Take a notecard with you today and jot down some of the thoughts that riddle your mind throughout the day.
- For a long time, my dominant thoughts were about scarcity in finances and opportunities and thinking about the future.

- Now that you are aware of your dominant thoughts, how can you be intentional about sowing something different?
- For example, when thoughts of money and finances come up I usually sing a little jingle that I remixed from one of my son's cartoons: "When you think about money STOP and pray right away." From there I remind myself that my father created the whole world and has great things planned for me.

Starve That Witch

"You have to starve that witch!"

She laughed and said, "What do you mean?"

I told her the story of Dr. Jekyll and Mrs. Hyde.

We all have a Jekyll and Hyde inside of us, and they are constantly at war. Jekyll represents all that is beneficial in life: hope, joy, peace, growth, fulfillment, patience, and love. Hyde represents all that is evil: anger, bitterness, jealousy, corruption, and fear.

For most of us Hyde eats at a buffet every day and gorges herself on steady supply of nutrients to grow big and strong.

On the other hand most of us feed Jekyll only table scraps and she is weak from lack of nutrition and water.

Then these two rage war inside of us and Jekyll continually gets beaten down to the point where we often give up on her completely.

Occasionally, we will bring Jekyll in from the cold and rain to let her eat at the buffet for a couple days or weeks, but never long enough for her to regain her full strength and win the war. Then we get mad and throw her back out in the cold and we refuse to believe in her.

In order to become the best version of ourselves and reach our greatest potential we must starve that which! We have to be mindful of everything we put into our heart: what we watch, listen to, read, our circle, our self-talk, and what we visualize, because all of those things are what Jekyll and Hyde feed off of.

Never forget to starve that witch!

TRAIN To Be Clutch

- Just because the battle is going on in your head does not mean that you are losing!
- You have the power to choose to intervene during the doubt storms in your life.
- Read *How To Stop The Pain* by James Richards
- Read *Crash The Chatterbox* by Steven Furtick

Comfortable vs. Content

It was all set up.

He hated his current circumstances. He hated his job. He hated that his girlfriend would never commit. He hated making less than minimum wage. He hated just about everything about his current life.

If only he would have stepped back to look at his options! He could have had the part-time job he had been asking about for years. He could have had a place to live. He could have lived in a city many people vacation in. He could have finally gotten away from the place he complained about and believed was holding him back.

BUT he was comfortable.

Have you ever noticed that some of us are comfortable being miserable?
We are comfortable doing average work.
We are more comfortable complaining instead of taking action.
We are comfortable not pursuing excellence.
We are comfortable enough to be inactive.

Comfortable is easy.
Comfortable never stretches you to grow.

Comfortable is rarely grateful.
Comfortable is complacent.
Comfortable is the enemy that wars against your greatest potential.

There is a big difference between comfortable and content.
Contentment is peace and joy where you are now.
Contentment is gratitude for what you *do* have.
Contentment will help you attract more resources and people to help make you better.

Learn to be content in all circumstances.

Avoid being comfortable.

He was miserable because he subconsciously wanted to be miserable. Deep down he didn't believe he deserved better. In his head he thought he deserved better, but in his heart he never believed it.

We are always doing what we want to do. There is always a choice, so we are always doing what we want to do.

If we wanted *it* as bad as we say we do, our lives would look very different because we would make radically different choices every day.

We Want Dessert Without the Desert

Looking back, I think I'm more grateful for the doors God has closed in my life than the ones He has opened.

When I was younger, I always wanted dessert before dinner. You see, I've never been great at knowing what is in my long-term best interest.

I might be older now, but I'm not sure much has changed. I think I still want dessert before dinner in many areas of my life.

When I was doing a volunteer internship at the Dream Center in Los Angeles, I brought the founder an idea he said was the best he had heard in 15 years. I put together a business plan with a very adept businessperson, and brought it back to the founder. I asked the Dream Center to put me on salary of $1,500 a month. I was told this wasn't possible because they were cutting expenses.

I was devastated at the time, and couldn't understand how this could happen. I was also REALLY frustrated with God. Rather than starting Dream Sports at the Dream Center, which had the infrastructure to facilitate the idea, I moved into the closet of a gym to try and start the smallest version of it at a local church with almost no infrastructure in place to support the idea.

Today, I'm so grateful the founder said no, because I wasn't ready for that type of role, and it wouldn't have been operating within my strengths. Not to mention, I wouldn't have been doing what I'm doing now, which I believe is my true passion and calling.

I wanted dessert, but what I really needed was some time alone in the desert. C.S. Lewis said, "Hardships often prepare ordinary people for an extraordinary destiny." But no one WANTS hardships, no one is seeking them out!

I see people quote Jeremiah 29:11 on Twitter all the time. You've probably seen it many times as well. "For I know the plans I have for you," declares the Lord, "plans to prosper you and not to harm you, plans to give you hope and a future." It's funny though, because I've NEVER seen Jeremiah 29:10 on Twitter. "When 70 years are complete...." Jeremiah was writing to people who were in exile, and would be for a total of SEVENTY YEARS!! We want verse 11 without going through verse 10.

We want the perks of the cool job without the responsibility and industriousness. Some of us want sex without the commitment of a relationship. We want the body without the diet and gym time. We want to be clutch without the sacrifice and training.

We want dessert without the desert.

As I look back at girlfriends, jobs, sports teams, and many other doors that have seemingly closed in my face for no reason, I'm incredibly grateful for them. I still struggle knowing what is in my best interest. Thankfully, God knows what is, and I'm content to be faithful with what He has placed in my hands, and trust He will close the doors that need to be closed regardless of my feelings.

TRAIN To Be Clutch

- What are some of the things that you wanted so badly in the past, that looking back you are glad did not work out?
- Maybe what we want right now isn't necessarily what we need.
- What are the resources and opportunities that you *do* have right now that you can be a great steward of?

What Are You Willing To Be Fired For?

"What do you believe in so strongly you are willing to be fired for it?"

I posed this question to a group of teachers in Birmingham, Alabama.

It is easy to tell students not to fall for peer pressure and to make the most beneficial choices, but how often do we model this behavior and fall for peer pressure as adults?

How often do we teach "to the test" out of the fear of losing our job?

How often do we focus on winning because our administration said if we don't make the tournament we will be fired?

How often do we focus on the bottom line and treat people like production units instead of people?

I told those teachers I hug the girls I work with, and I tell them I love them when I feel it is appropriate. I understand that this might get me fired one day, but I am willing to get fired for what I believe.

I learned as a nine year old when I pulled my best friend and baby brother out of our pool that life is fragile and very short. We aren't guaranteed tomorrow.

As I write this, I'm not guaranteed to make it to our game this evening versus Colorado. I could die before I get there, BUT the one thing I do know is that the girls I mentor know beyond a shadow of a doubt that I love them, that I'm proud of them, and that I believe the very best in them.

They know this because I am not afraid to live out what I believe in their life.

We want to encourage you to be courageous. What do you believe in? Do people know this by the way you live, or do you have to tell them?

Think back to a time when you showed unbelievable courage for what you believed in. If you believe in learning rather than teaching to the test, are you willing to get fired for living that out? If you believe in falling in love with the process of becoming great rather than focusing on outcomes in games, are you willing to get fired for living that out?

The reason we love and admire people like MLK, Ghandi, and Abraham Lincoln is not because they are extraordinary men with God-like qualities. We love them because they were ordinary people who were willing to die for living out extraordinary principles.

TRAIN To Be Clutch

- List out some of the things that you are passionate about. What are the "Yeah, but..." thoughts that come up as roadblocks to your dreams?
- When people tell you that something can't be done because of _____, ask yourself "Who says?" and see if those roadblocks are just obstacles that steer us toward creative solutions.

Blame vs. Responsibility

"It wasn't my fault!"

"He is the one to blame."

"It's HER fault!"

"The government is to blame!"

We hear these phrases every single day. *The ironic part of blame is that while it might temporarily make us feel better, it does absolutely nothing towards creating a better tomorrow.*

We love it when a person coaching in the NFL steps up to the podium after a tough loss and doesn't blame the people reffing, the conditions, or worse, blame his team. We love when they take responsibility for making things better, AND here is the catch, REGARDLESS of who was to blame.

We can take responsibility even when we aren't to blame for the situation, but it takes a very secure and confident person to do this.

If you are the leader of a group of people, taking responsibility is one of the most powerful things you can do to create resilient allegiance in your troops. If you are a part of the troops, taking responsibility is the quickest way to gain the respect and trust of leadership. *Anyone can blame, very few have the courage to take responsibility.*

Remember, blame is about the past. Responsibility is about the present and future.

It's easy to blame the government.
It's hard to take responsibility for our community and make a difference even if it is in just one person's life.

It's easy to blame your teammate for turning the ball over on the last possession of the game.
It's hard to be in the best shape of your life, and put up 250 made free throws while visualizing you are in a pressure packed situation EVERY SINGLE DAY.

It's easy to blame your team for not playing hard and not caring enough.
It's hard to take responsibility for the team you are leading and make sure they are better prepared from now on.

It's easy to blame the Democrats or Republicans for shutting down the government.
It's hard to find what unites us and work together to create solutions.

It's easy to blame.
It's hard to take responsibility....especially when it's not *our* fault.

If you learn to give credit, and take responsibility at every opportunity you will be on the fast track to becoming a great leader who is able to mobilize people to accomplish amazing feats. You will build incredible relationships in the process.

Are You Undercutting Your Work?

When you punish people for making a mistake or falling short of a goal, you create an environment of extreme caution, even fearfulness. In sports it's similar to playing "not to lose—a formula that often brings on defeat." —John Wooden

If you are reading this book, then there is no doubt you are serious about improving your game, becoming a better parent, or sharpening your skills for work. You are probably putting in extra work after training with your team, reading blogs and books to help expand your knowledge, going home and doing extra running shooting, passing and dribbling to make sure that you get better. I love that you are striving to get better, but I wonder if you are practicing as effectively as possible?

As I train people across the country I fear somewhere around 40-60% of their training and education is being undercut or robbed of its effectiveness. Sadly, the culprit lies within each individual. I wonder if you are much different?

Let me tell you one of my own stories. One day I was out doing a tough 30 minute interval run. In this run I'm not trying to cover a particular amount of ground, but I am just trying to run as hard as I can during each segment. That day I was working extremely hard and I really broke through a few barriers. My lungs were burning and my legs were hurting but every time I got tired I simply ran harder.

It was a great workout to say the least, but when I finished, the thoughts that hit me sounded like this:

"I bet Shane would have done that run better. I bet Tyson would have covered more ground and he wouldn't have been as tired as I am. You barely got through that workout. Your face was showing the struggle the whole time and guys who are fit don't look like that when they run. All the guys in the league would have done better than that. The guys on the national team would have covered way more ground than you."

It took me a second, but I just laughed. I just did all of that work and then I tried to undercut everything I did! And the thoughts were not based on facts. They were false constructs or stories I had created out of nowhere! Lies Lies Lies!!!

Do you ever do something similar?

Recently I went back and tried to estimate how many hours of practice I have accumulated over the years. I calculated that by the time I was 18 years old I had around 8,000 hours of practice under my belt. Considering the rule of thumb that it takes a minimum of 10,000 hours of deliberate practice to become an expert at anything, I should have had all the results and confidence in the world. Sadly, I truly believe that only around 3,000 of those hours were as effective as they could have been, because the majority of the time I kept focusing on false constructs:

"Those kids in Chicago are probably putting in harder work than me and they have better resources available to them."

"Those kids in England have better drills than I do and better opportunities."

The more I focused on those things, the worse I felt at my sport and as a person and in turn, the less I focused on how I could get better.

Sound familiar? Go ahead and evaluate your self-talk after a meeting, practice, presentation, or at the end of the day. So how can we change it?

A guy named Mark Batterson wrote something that has changed my life. He says, "Success is doing the best you can with what you have where you are." And he is right. When I started going into workouts and games with that mindset, that all I can do is control my effort and do the best I can, everything changed for me. If and when those negative thoughts came up I just focused on true mental toughness and controllables in that moment.

You cannot control what other people have done in the past or are doing right now. You cannot control the resources and coaching that you have had in the past. All that is in your control is how you execute in the present moment.

We have to talk to ourselves instead of listening to ourselves. If we listen to ourselves we are most likely going to hear all of the reasons we cannot do something. We will direct our focus and energy towards things outside of our control instead of controlling our focus and energy.

TRAIN To Be Clutch

- As you go into training or work this week, write out your performance cue card. At the end of the day, evaluate your self-talk and circle things that you don't think are the most beneficial things to say. Then focus the next day on more beneficial things to sow in your heart.

- Realize that you can only control the controllables in the present moment, and aim for growth. And don't forget to laugh at the ridiculous thoughts that try to flood your mind. They make for great stories down the road!

Our Greatest Fear

"Our greatest fear should not be of failure but of succeeding at things in life that don't really matter." — Francis Chan

We put so much emphasis on winning in our culture, it makes me wonder if one day we will get to the top of the ladder and realize our ladder was on the wrong building.

When I ask people, who operate in many varied contexts, to write out what they want to be remembered for when they leave the earth, NO ONE writes down how many championships they won or how much money they made.

Being faced with death has a powerful way of stripping away the insignificant and leaving only what truly matters. During the obituary exercise most people tell us they want to be known for their personal characteristics and having deep and meaningful relationships. *At our core, deep in our heart, when we move aside all the junk that distracts us, we know what it looks like to put first things first.* It's interesting how our deathbeds have a way making us realize what is actually important.

Steve Jobs put it this way; "Remembering that I'll be dead soon is the most important tool I've ever encountered to help me make the big choices in life. Almost everything—all external expectations, all pride, all fear of embarrassment or failure—these things just fall away in the face of death, leaving only what is truly important."

When I entered my senior year of undergrad my father was diagnosed with stage-four cancer. I watched as the priorities in his life radically shifted, and his appreciation for the little things grew rapidly.

This was a man who grew up in a trailer park where he had to duct-tape his family trailer to keep it from falling apart. With a lot of hard work and unflappable persistence he went from being a drug dealer as a teenager to becoming one of the most successful eye surgeons in Oklahoma.

My father knew about success.
He lived the American Dream.
He was an example that social mobility still exists in our country.

However, I couldn't help but wonder if he had known he would only live to be 51 years old if he would have done things differently.

I know for sure he would have been A LOT more grateful in life and treated people close to him radically different.

I made a commitment after he got cancer that I wouldn't wait until I got cancer to appreciate everything God had given me in life.

I hope my focus is always succeeding at receiving God's unconditional love, loving God, loving myself, loving others, serving people, providing value, encouraging and equipping people. I can do those things regardless of what field I'm in, or what I'm most passionate about. ***I want to be able to honestly look back on my deathbed and know I put first things first and did my best to succeed at what really matters in life.***

What Do John Wooden and Pete Carroll Have In Common?

I tell people in leadership all the time.

"Don't bitch
Don't beg
Enforce healthy boundaries with love and respect."

One of my favorite stories is when Bill Walton showed up to the bus for an away game with facial hair. John Wooden communicated to his team that their hair be neat and tidy. He told Walton that his hair looked great, but that unfortunately he couldn't play on the team with that hair.

If it were me, I think it would have been easy to compromise in this situation with the guy who is the best in the country. "We are stopping at the first CVS and you are buying shaving cream and a razor WITH YOUR OWN MONEY!!!"

How many of us would yell at the person who is the star of our team and tell them how disappointed we are in their lack of discipline and leadership?

Wooden was willing to potentially sacrifice a game for his principles, and he left Walton off the bus to figure out how to get to the game on his on, with a proper haircut. But he did it in a way that treated Walton with love and respect.

He enforced a healthy boundary, which is one of the best ways to teach and bring out the best in those we lead.

It's tempting to nag people about what we want them to do, but nagging and bitching is only reinforcing the very behaviors we say we don't want more of. If we really want to influence behavior, we are responsible for enforcing healthy boundaries with love and respect.

Jamie tells the story about an incident that changed his life. One of his responsibilities growing up was to clean the kitchen and do the dishes. His mom was continually getting on to him about having it done before she got home from work. One day she enforced a healthy boundary. She told him that if the dishes were not cleaned before she came home, he would not be allowed to go to practice. He didn't heed the boundary. She didn't let him go to practice. When the guy coaching Jamie's team saw him the next week he relayed the message that Jamie had let his team down.

Let's just say that the kitchen was spotless for the next 6 years. No bitching. No begging. Just an enforced healthy boundary.

In studies on married couples it has been shown that you get more of what you focus on. So, what should you do? Praise the heck out of what you want. *If a person on your team does something well, then make a big deal out of it.* Continue to catch them doing it well!

Killer whales are trained with 100% positive reinforcement because you can't punish a killer whale. Their trainers ignore their bad behavior and reward them when they do what the trainers want them to do.

Pete Carroll has long been known for using positive reinforcement with the guys on his team and he is one of a select few people in coaching to have won a Super Bowl and a BCS national championship.

Sometimes it's hard to write a thank you card when someone does something small and you think you deserve SO MUCH more, but writing the thank you card is a much better way of getting MORE of that behavior in the future.

Encourage what you want.
Stop bitching.
Stop begging.

Enforce healthy boundaries with love and respect, and you just might wake up one day to realize you are bringing out the very best in those around you.

Your Context Is Your Training Ground For Who You Are Becoming

People often come to me after a difficult day dejected and frustrated.

One of the first questions I ask them is *"were you intentional about making someone's day great today?"*

"No Jamie, you didn't hear me. Things didn't go well for *me* today!"

"No I heard you clearly. *But did you hear me?* Name a person for whom you went out of your way to make their day great."

It's after that second go around that they get it. Usually, **when things don't feel great in our lives, we stop thinking about other people**. The world becomes OUR world as though it was made for me, not you. We narrow our focus in on how things are conspiring against us at every turn.

I get it, in a round of golf, a business meeting, or wherever you find yourself day to day, it's hard to focus on making someone's day great. It's counter-cultural. It's seldom rewarded. But it's really not even about that. It's about who you are becoming.

I work with a guy who is 15 and plays golf. He gets frustrated in the same way. But during our time together we have unpacked the type of person that he wants to become. Though golf is important and he wants to play professionally, he is choosing to *use* golf as a training ground for who he is becoming.

Two things are on his list. He wants to pursue excellence in everything he does, and he wants to make others feel the love of Jesus by the way he treats them.

Here's how he does both.

First, part of pursuing excellence is training the ability to narrow your focus. If a round of golf takes five hours, one will quickly wear himself out if he is trying to focus for the entire 300 minutes. Movies are only between 90-120 minutes for a reason! Most of us struggle to focus for longer than that.

What we decided is that this young man would start to play *"glove to glove."*

When he puts his glove on before a shot, that is his cue to narrow his focus on the process. After he hits it, he thinks about it and asks, "If I could do it again, how would I do it differently?" Then when he hears that Velcro of the glove unstrapping, he moves his focus to the other people he is playing with.

If the group he is with isn't very chatty, he then shifts his focus to a one square-foot piece of grass and thinks about how insane it is that God knows each blade of grass and he can't even count them! (He came up with that one on his own!!!!)

It isn't easy. It's not being modeled. It's certainly not his default. But golf is finally becoming much more enjoyable for him and he is performing much better on the course as well.

Most importantly, my friend is learning that golf, school, business, relationships, and anything he does are all training grounds for the person he wants to become. That is using your sport!

In what ways would it benefit us to break up our day having periods where we zoom in and narrow our focus on what we are doing, and then broaden it for a bit to gain a different perspective?

As a dad working from home, I found it insanely frustrating to be constantly interrupted by flying play dough and foam golf balls, as awesome as that is!

But now I practice honing in on writing, and then pulling out for periods of intentional time with my son and my wife.

For people coaching, maybe there need to be points in your day where you pull out of your intense focus on admin work and video and narrow in to listen, I mean put the phone down and *genuinely* listen to the people that you *get to* lead.

Maybe in our job it could be insanely beneficial to have points where we come up for air to read an article, go for a gratefulness walk, speak with a friend, or practice some deep breathing.

What I know is that if we keep trying to go at break neck speed throughout the entire day with a hawk-eye focus, most of us are going to miss out on things that are truly important in life.

The only things that matter about your day are who you are becoming and the influence you have on others.

TRAIN To Be Clutch

- Identify 2-5 points in your day where you can choose to zoom out from the task at hand.
- During that time, reflect on how your task is training the characteristics you want to adopt.

Perverted Humility

I don't often see people in their late sixties get choked up easily, and when the grandmother of a girl playing golf I had just spoken to had tears in her eyes, I realized how deep her pain really went. She had just tried to tell me about the importance of *humility*, at least what she had been told was humility. The story went like this...

"My father always made sure we never got a big head and stayed humble. I can vividly remember coming home from school one day and telling him about how my friends had told me how pretty I was. He looked at me and said, they must not have been wearing their glasses."

As she was saying this she got choked up from the stomach, not just tears, but she made a movement like she was actually about to vomit. She said, "I guess it still hurts."

I hope to never experience something like that.

Is this humility? In my opinion it is the farthest thing from it. What kind of father unconditionally loves their daughter by telling them something like that, and then tells them that is humility? The pain from those words has left an infected wound forty plus years later. Does that perverted humility help her accomplish her dreams or help her realize she is a precious child of God? Does it help guide her to a place where she can truly love and edify others?

NO.

It is the most perverted form of humility around. Everywhere I speak this same notion always pops up. "What about humility, what about humility? Are you teaching kids to be cocky?" If this is what you call humility, shattering dreams and self-esteem, then I want absolutely nothing to do with it.

People tend to do things they are proud of when they are in a healthy state of mind, and you typically feel that way after someone has spent time speaking life into your heart. It is great when other people do it for you, but we can also do it for ourselves. Especially when there are people out there perverting humility and sowing death into invaluable hearts and minds.

I think the Harvard Business Review article, "How Will You Measure Your Life?" by Clayton M. Christensen summarizes humility well.

"I got this insight when I was asked to teach a class on humility at Harvard College. I asked all the students to describe the most humble person they knew. One characteristic of these humble people stood out: They had a high level of self-esteem. They knew who they were and they felt good about who they were. We also decided that humility was defined not by self-deprecating behavior or attitudes but by the esteem with which you regard others. Good behavior flows naturally from that kind of humility."

True humility is believing you can do anything you set your mind to and being willing to confidently take steps toward your dreams knowing that you were meticulously created for a purpose. It is being confident in who you are and whose you are, so you can help others see who they were created to be.

Are You Waiting On Your Moment Or Training For Your Moment?

"How hard are you going to train when you get to your college team?"

I was talking with a high school sophomore who had already committed to a D1 school to play basketball. He told me he was going to be the hardest worker on the team and be committed to putting in more hours of training than anyone else.

I then asked the tough question, "Is that how you use your time now?"

Silence on the other end of the phone....

....

....

....

Much less confident now he says, "No, not even close. I guess I've just been waiting for the opportunity to get here to change my habits. I mean, I work hard, don't get me wrong, but I know I'll have to work twice as hard to compete at the D1 level."

You see, I think we all fall into that trap at times in our life.

When I make more money, THEN I will financially support the causes I believe are worthy.

When I get a better office, THEN I will have a better attitude towards work.

When I get paid what I deserve, THEN I will have a great attitude, treat people really, really well, give my very, very best, and have unconditional gratitude, regardless of my circumstances.

When I become a starter for my team, THEN I will be the first in, last out.

When I get different people on my team, then I will apply the *Train to be CLUTCH* tools.

When I turn pro, THEN I will take mental training seriously.

When I get out of college, THEN I will start pursuing my dream.

The list could go on and on. The trouble is, if you are waiting on your moment, when the moment arrives you won't be prepared. **While you were waiting, many others were training.**

When the moment arrives, only those who have been training and expecting the day to arrive will be ready to seize the opportunity. And truthfully those people tend to create and attract many of those opportunities to them BECAUSE they've been training to their max rather than waiting for their moment.

It's so easy to say, "When this or that happens, THEN I will change." But **the greatest indicator of our future behavior is our past** *behavior.* It's not that your future is dictated by your past. We can all change and grow. But *if you don't change now, it will be twice as hard then.*

The question we must ask ourselves every day is, *"How would I use my 86,400 seconds today if I knew I was going to get the opportunity of my dreams?!"*

If you want to achieve your greatest potential, you must fall in love with the process of becoming great, especially when your dreams are so far away you can barely catch a glimpse of them.

The opportunity will come.

Will you be ready?

What Actually Happened Doesn't Really Matter

"So tell me your thoughts on your season," I said.

"Well...." She took a deep breath, "we had the worst season ever in our program's history. We were the first team to not make the conference tournament. We were the first team to have a losing record. So, yeah, it was pretty bad."

Smiling I said, **"So you're feeling like a failure, right?"**

"Oh yeah," she said dejectedly.

I had a hunch there were some great things that happened this year she was forgetting to mention. I had spoken with her before the season and she was not sure if she was even going to touch the field this year. So I asked about how she played and it turns out that she started *every* game and played almost *every* minute! How could she miss that?

I did a workshop with a high school basketball team recently and I asked all the guys to write out 15 specific things they did well after practice. You've never seen such struggle in your life! About 5 minutes into it I asked, "How many you have left?"

"5, 8, 3" they said. And just when they thought I would say that they could finish it later, with a smile I said, "Keep going."

You see, what I have come to find out is that for the most part, we are horrible at self-evaluation. As humans we have a negativity bias that colors the way we remember events in our lives. We tend to forget the things that we do well and focus on and blow up the mistakes that we make. And usually, we buy into the idea that mistakes = identity.

As they finished up, I asked who was still working and there was one guy who had one left. So I asked the team, "Will someone please tell him something he did well today?"
His buddy turns and says, "You knocked down a clutch three on the base line during the transition drill."
With a look of confusion, he quipped back, "No I didn't!"
Then three more people on the team confirmed exactly what happened: "This is who you got the pass from, this is where you were, and this is what happened right after." With a look of embarrassment he said, "Well...I think my feet were on the line, though."

ARE YOU KIDDING ME!!!! First of all you can't even remember that you scored. Secondly, you are willing to explain away half of the points you scored that day! And you say you want to help the team????

Now, there are people who have the reverse challenge and can't see that they are doing some things wrong, but the fact that you are reading this book means that you are probably not that type of person. But please don't miss this:
It doesn't necessarily matter what actually happened; what matters is how we explain it to ourselves.

Did you have a poor season? Ok, keep telling yourself that and forget about all the indicators of growth. Did you have a poor birdie putt? Great, never mind the excellent drive and approach that got you there. Did you miss a last second shot? Super, let's wipe our memory clean of the other 37 minutes of hard nosed defense and stellar passing.

I'll share my wife's most hated phrase:

Your choice creates *your* challenge!

The great thing about it is that how you explain things is **completely inside of your control.**

So you want to change the way you tend to think? You want to grow for the next game, practice and season? Try this after every practice, game, and season:
- Write out: "My worth does not come from what I do, it comes from who I am"
- Write out 15-63 *specific* things that you did well
- Write out 2 areas for growth
- Write out 2-3 things that you learned
- Write out the Growth Mindset Creedo: "Anything that happens to me today is in my best interest. It's an opportunity to learn and grow."

*"Anything that happens to me today is in my best interest because it **CAN** make me a better person and better at my craft"*

Notice I said *can*. It doesn't just happen automatically. It comes from a **consistent intentionality** to explain things in the most beneficial way possible!

If you think this is hard work, well tell that to the 9 year-old I train whom after practice wrote out 32 things he did well. It only took him 42 minutes. That's commitment!

This training tool has elicited more growth in people, teams, and organizations than almost anything else we do. Our memories are not formed from our experience, our memories are formed from the retelling of events, which means the stories we tell ourselves and others are what actually form our memories.

You don't need someone coaching to help you do this. It's the responsibility of someone coaching to teach you to grow; but your responsibility is taking ownership of your development by tracking how you are growing. So please, do this simple exercise!

Or...disregard everything I just said. Don't evaluate yourself in the most beneficial manner. Don't take 5 minutes after you play to make sure you get the most out of your session. Don't take a vested interest in growing at your craft and as a person.

Really, the choice is yours. And, you guessed it: **Your choice creates Your challenge!**

CHAPTER

Dirty Hard Work

"Everyone thinks that greatness is sexy, it's not. It is dirty hard work." -Ben Hogan

Calling all 180 people responsible for leading the golf programs attending the WGCA conference we were speaking at was not easy, especially when we only had 5 days before the event. It was a simple strategy, but it was *dirty hard work*.

A lot of people are looking for a complex strategy, a new system, or some other fancy plan to help them succeed. The reality is, that it is a commitment to doing the dirty hard work that is going to get you where you want to go. It's not complex or fancy. It is a commitment to doing the dirty work that is going to help you mold and shape your character into the person you want to become. It's simple stuff, but simple isn't easy.

It wasn't a complex marketing strategy to call all 180 people before the event. It was countercultural to not try and sell them anything. All we did was ask them "What is you mission in coaching? What is your mission for your program? We are here to serve you, so let us know if there is anything we can do to help you, regardless of whether you can ever hire us out to work with your program. We create lots of free tools for people every week, and we just want to equip you in anyway we can."

We were told no one had ever called all the people before the event and not tried to sell them anything. The people who called were always trying to sell them something. Never had the people who were giving one of the main talks taken the time to call. It is dirty hard work. One of the guys apologized for not calling us back, "I'm so sorry for not calling you back, I thought the ladies on my team were playing a practical joke on me. I didn't think there was anyway you guys were actually calling every coach here." We were getting up 3 hours earlier than normal and staying up later in order to call every person attending, while still handling our day-to-day responsibilities. We also called all the people in assistant coach positions.

Was it incredibly hard? Yes.

Did we want to give up at times? Yes.

Were some of the people very rude to us? Yes.

Did Jamie almost lose his voice? Yes.

Was it worth it? Most definitely!!!

We built some incredible relationships, and as a byproduct of doing the dirty hard work and actually caring about the people, many teams have asked us to come out for workshops and keynotes. We put first things first, and second things were not suppressed. Second things increased!

TRAIN To Be Clutch

- What are some actions that are 100% under your control that you could be faithful in doing?
- What are most other people on your team or in your field not willing to do?
- How much growth could you experience by having a willingness to do the dirty hard work?

CHAPTER

The Same Excuse

Many people feel like the fundamentals are no longer important, and they would rather play games than build the foundational skills. It frustrates them that the people coaching their teams are "out of touch" and don't understand the *modern* game. This drives most people in leadership crazy and they can't believe they have to put up with people who think they know better than the ones responsible for leading the team. The people on their team don't understand all the wisdom the people coaching have and how much better they would be if they spent the majority of their time developing their fundamental skills.

But here is the interesting thing: people in leadership often hide behind a similar excuse.

When I tell people in leadership what John Wooden did, they make excuses and say, "we live in a different time, and his methods are out of touch with our current reality in the coaching world." They never outright say he is wrong, but they always try and justify putting winning at the top of their priority list. Winning has become the priority in their minds, because it is the "reality" for the people in coaching today, and their livelihood is riding on results.

The excuses look very similar to me. People coaching today are looking at Wooden saying, "you are out of touch, and your methods wouldn't work today" and people are looking at the men and women leading their program saying "playing ball is more important than the fundamentals of the past." Whether it is a person playing or leading, those excuses become stories that they tell themselves. **The stories we tell ourselves become our beliefs, and our beliefs become the lens through which we see the world.**

Our brains are processing 200 million bits of information every second, but we are only aware of 2,000 of those bits, or .0001% of our "reality." People coaching see this everyday with how "blind" the people on their team are to how deficient their game is because of a lack of fundamentals. I wonder if John Wooden was still here if he would see the same thing in modern coaching with people leading who place winning over the process.

Ultimately, true mental toughness is a higher standard than winning. So why are we afraid of making that the standard?! If our focus is true mental toughness and doing our best to grow from every experience, the results will ultimately be better than if we are focused on winning. If we are focused on winning we will develop holes in our foundation that will eventually crack under pressure. In the very same manner, a person's game will eventually crack under pressure if they don't develop their fundamentals. What is needed is for the people leading teams and the people they lead to realize that the wisdom of the greats that have gone before us is still applicable today. And adherence to that wisdom is crucial for tapping into our greatest potential.

Live According to Principles Or Live According To Circumstances

If I were to ask you to list out the five guiding principles in your life, what would they be? Could you even do it?

In my time mentoring people I've found that way too many of us are living according to circumstances. Others are living according to principles, and that is the type of person I want to become.

One of the ladies I have trained for the last year called me extremely frustrated with her game. She was not hitting the ball as well as she was used to hitting it and her scores and the team's scores were struggling.

During our time together we talk about principles that we are choosing to live our life by. Here are some examples:

- Anything that happens to me today is in my best interest, it's an opportunity to learn and grow.
- Do the best you can with what you have where you are.
- Excellent body language can trump emotional feelings.
- Trust your gut.

- If I abide in Him and His words abide in me, I can ask anything of the Father and He will provide it.
- What CAN you do?
- Talk to yourself instead of listening to yourself.
- October is coming.
- God is not surprised. God is sovereign.
- Value listening more than being listened to.
- Sometimes things are less about you and more about other people.
- I know that You, God, can do all things and that no plan of yours can be thwarted.
- The only thing that matters today is who I become and the influence I have on other people.
- Everyone was created in God's image. Treat them according to who they are, not what they do.
- My value comes from who I am, not what I do.
- Pursue excellence no matter what.
- Sometimes you have to say F your feelings and choose to be excellent.

These are examples of some of my guiding principles and I encourage people to write down their own principles in the morning. Start with five and add one more each week.

These principles sound great on paper, but most of us do not reinforce them regularly. When the storms come and the boat is being rocked, most of us panic and succumb to our emotions. That's circumstantial living.

So my friend, as hard as it was, was trying to focus on principles in the midst of a crazy storm in life. It wasn't easy. There were times where she was wondering what was wrong with her. Was she a sub-par human being? Why couldn't she figure it out?!

About two months later we jumped on a call and I asked her to share something great that had happened recently. She said her mom was in town and they went out to play golf together. Her mom was looking at her clubs and said, "Honey, your clubs are all bent differently."

"What!?! No I got them re-fitted two months ago."

Upon further inspection, she realized that all of her irons were bent to different degrees.

"No wonder I couldn't hit anything consistently!!!! This whole time I thought there was something wrong with *me*!"

She sent the clubs back and got things straightened out and is now playing much more consistently. I don't really care about the result on the course. What I care about is that she was training the ability to live according to principles instead of feelings. If she didn't have those principles in her heart, I am not sure what would have happened.

If we are not thoughtful about the principles that guide our lives, then when the inevitable storms in our life come we are left to react to our emotions.

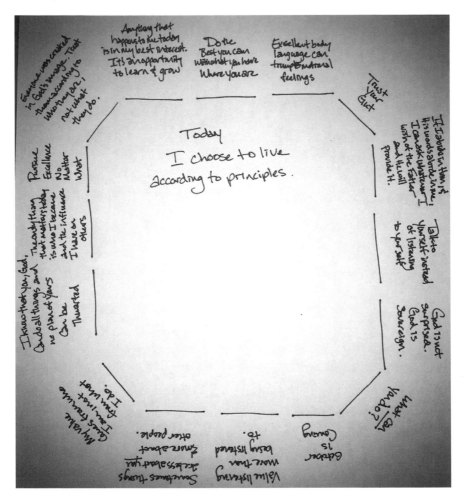

Almost every morning I start of my day by writing sixteen principles in a circle. Many of these principles stay the same but some change. But the circle is important to me. I imagine that those principles are the ropes and posts in a boxing ring. If I have those set, then when I face huge obstacles in life, the principles keep me in the fight.

TRAIN To Be Clutch

- List out 5-10 principles that you would like to guide your life.

- For the next week, write out these principles in a circle early on in your day.
- As storms come in your day, recite these principles or write them down.

Use The Pain

Turn your wounds into wisdom. –Oprah

Fear and ignorance are pervasive throughout our society.

The board at Apple ran out Steve Jobs after he created the company.

The "business experts" tried to run out Mark Zuckerberg from Facebook, saying he wasn't qualified to run the company he created.

The South African government called Nelson Mandela a terrorist and held him in prison for over 30 years.

Some people still believe African Americans aren't fit for serving in head coaching positions or playing quarterback on a football team.

Some people still think women aren't fit to run a company.

Condoleeza Rice's dad always told her, you might have to be 2 or 3 times as good, but no one can stop you.

People crucified Jesus.

They killed Martin Luther King Jr.

They tried to kill Ghandi.

So, rest assured, we are going to experience "haters." We are going to run into people who are threatened by us, and they are going to throw down the gauntlet in front of us....USE it!

They are throwing down an obstacle course of challenges, but if we embrace it and run through it, we will become stronger and better because of it. Believe everything that happens to you is in your best interest and an opportunity to learn and grow. Use those challenges as an opportunity to develop even more true mental toughness. Have a great attitude. Give your very very best. Treat people really, really well. Have unconditional gratitude. Even when you think your circumstances suck.

They can't stop you. They can only make it harder for you. Only *you* can stop you.

Keep the faith. Be courageous. Use the pain.

If it is raining, bottle the water and sell it. If crap falls from the sky, package it and sell fertilizer. If it is sunny, put out your vegetables to grow a garden. No matter what happens, use it.

It feels good to hear "you're brilliant" but it doesn't really make me better. It might increase my confidence, but it isn't going to sharpen me. When I run from criticism or the tough stuff, I miss out on the opportunity to stretch and grow. The first year I worked with UCLA women's basketball program was one of the toughest groups I've ever worked with, and it made me so much better. The following year it was one of the greatest groups of kids I have ever had the pleasure of training, but I would have missed out on that experience if I ran when it got tough.

Remember, our dreams are on the other side of our challenges.
Planes take off *against* the wind, not with it.
Strength is only built through resistance.

You can download or listen to the mp3 of this chapter here.

TRAIN To Be Clutch

- What pain do you have in life right now that you would really benefit from using instead of running from it?
- In what areas of your life do you feel like it is pouring rain, and how could you bottle the water and sell it?
- Everyone wants to shine like a diamond, but who wants to go through a 2,000 degree furnace, and then have the weight of 7,000 grown men on top of you, AND then, after all that, be cut and polished?
- Changing your language from "the problem is" to "the challenge is" or "the opportunity is" is a simple way to change perspective and habitual action over time.

Every Now And Then vs. A Lifestyle

I was reading one of Jon Gordon's books on a Southwest flight when all of a sudden I looked up and there was a very large man asking me if I wanted peanuts or pretzels. This guy didn't look like a flight attendant; he looked like he belonged in an Under Armour commercial! His body was the size of one of those manikins they put the football jerseys on.

The crazy part was this guy must have been over 55 years old. It got me thinking: I wonder if anyone would look at this guy and say, "Man, he *must* have been born that way!" No way! It is obvious this guy is meticulous about his diet and working out. The evidence is overwhelming. He doesn't have to tell anyone on the street that he works out. Everyone for blocks knows it!

Sometimes we look at people who have qualities and character we admire and we so easily write it off as if they were born that way. It is true we are all born with different attributes, but where we start doesn't determine where we finish. Most people who have the characteristics we admire refined those over a long period of time through *deliberate* and *intentional* choices day after day after day.

When it comes to molding and shaping our personal characteristics we are like the person who is only in the gym from January 3rd until January 15th who complains that diets and exercise don't work. We pick up a book like, Mindset, every now and then. We are deliberate *occasionally*. We live by our principles *sometimes*. Then we wonder why we get *sometimes* and *occasional* results.

If you want to experience the benefits of mental training, it has to be a commitment to a certain lifestyle. It can't just be an every now and then thing. Especially in the beginning, because it takes so much energy to make changes and turn things around in your life. But have you ever pushed past the point of exhaustion, the point where you think you can't give any more? Have you ever smiled and pushed past that temporary pain to see what is on the other side? The amount of energy it takes to get your plane in the air is immense, but once it is in the air you have more freedom.

In college we laughed when people told us they worked out, because we knew they might work out every now and then, but they most likely had no clue what it was like to go through a Mark Davis workout! We were being pushed past what we thought was humanly possible on a daily basis.

I love to watch the faces on people in our workshops when Jamie asks the question, "How many books do you read in a day?" People look like they just bit into a sour fruit, because they didn't even know that was a real measurement.

Most people will do visualization exercises for five minutes every now and then.
Most people will pick up a transformational book every now and then.
Most people will be intentional in how they treat people every now and then.
Most people will give their very best in training every now and then.

And they wonder why they don't get the results they are looking for?!!!

If you want to look like an Under Armour mannequin you must be committed to a certain type of lifestyle. If you want to fulfill your greatest potential you must be committed to a certain type of lifestyle. That doesn't mean you won't miss days or slip up at times; but it means you are willing to say yes to the toughest stuff the majority of the time.

If you want to tap into your greatest potential...
If you want to become everything you are capable of becoming....
If you want to become the type of person you want to become....

It must become a lifestyle.

You must start visualizing playing at your best and overcoming the inevitable obstacles before EVERY practice and before EVERY game.

You must start studying and training like a student in medical school.

You must start visualizing walking into the test full of energy, confidence, and remembering everything you have studied.

You must start visualizing walking into the boardroom full of confidence, and handling every potential obstacle with poise and grace.

Mental training must become a lifestyle rather than an every now and then thing. And when you do this consistently over time everyone around you will start to be able to SEE the difference in you. Just like the flight attendant on my flight, you won't have to tell anyone about the changes you've made; they will be more than evident by the way you live and who you have become.

Where You Start Doesn't Determine Where You FINISH

I have a hunch...

My hunch is that if you told Tiger Woods he was talented I think he would, and I argue he potentially should, take offense to that statement.

Hidden beneath statements like these is the idea that certain people are born with something the rest of us just weren't born with, AND the preposterous idea that they didn't have to acquire tens of thousands of hours of hard and often painful deliberate practice to develop their skills. In essence, the idea being articulated is that a talented person didn't have to work very hard to get where they are at now. It kind of matches the shirt that reads "Talented but lazy."

Quite frankly, I think this is a really convenient excuse for most people to believe.

Earl Woods started doing purposeful visualization with Tiger before baby Tiger was able to walk. Earl would put Tiger in a baby swing and had him watch as he hit balls into a net for hours in their garage. Earl also happened to be a pretty good golfer, with a good swing. He understood Tiger would start to develop the neurological pathways for a golf swing by watching all those hours of swinging a club. Remember, muscle memory isn't actually wrapped in our muscles; it is wrapped in our brains. By the time Tiger was ten years old, and at the very latest by 13, he had acquired over ten thousand hours of deliberate practice.

Deliberate practice is radically different than how many of us practice. Most of us don't go until exhaustion and then push harder. We don't consistently seek out challenges that are just out of our grasp. And most of us are not intentional about the mechanics of what we are training. Deliberate practice is a constant stretching of one's abilities and the attempting of feats just outside your ability. It is hard, often lonely, and intensely draining, which is why so few people acquire enough of it to make a difference. The cool part is it doesn't matter if we are talking sports, education, music, parenting, or business skills. Deliberate practice is what makes all the difference.

Any skill can be developed, and the earlier you start to practice deliberately, the better off you will be. Studies have shown human capacity for wrapping muscle memory (myelin) is greater when you are under sixteen years old, but that it is possible at any age.

One thing is clear when it comes to talent, whether it is Kobe Bryant, Tiger Woods, Lebron James, or the best in any business, when you get behind the scenes it becomes very obvious why they became the best in the world. People who have failed to make their dreams come true love to preach about the importance of talent and warn anyone within earshot about all the factors outside of their control that are necessary to achieve excellence.

However, when you study the tops of their fields, a very different picture presents itself. The people who achieve sustained excellence tend to have relentless work ethic and a willingness to delay satisfaction for long periods of time. They have fallen in love with the process, and are constantly seeking out better strategies to continue to get better. In essence you find they have a strong belief in constant and never-ending improvement.

I often have people tell me about my "gift" and "talent" for public speaking and it really bothers me. Do I have an anointing when I speak? I would say without a doubt! But a gift? I would argue with that.

Let me give you a little background.

I am extremely introverted, but I have been doing speaking engagements since I was 12 years old. I also have a communications degree. I was trained by one of the best speech teachers in the world, and I ran a network marketing company where I was presenting in front of groups every week for six months. Let me share a secret with you, I STILL GET EXTREMELY NERVOUS about talking in groups when I'm not in control! I give keynotes in front of thousands of people, yet in a small group when asked to share my name and my favorite color my palms start to sweat and I get butterflies in my stomach. Why does that make me nervous? I DON'T KNOW! But I do know that public speaking is not a gift of mine. It is a skill that I have developed over many years of deliberate practice and putting myself in situations to stretch and grow.

One of the other reasons it looks like I have a gift of public speaking is because of how well I know the information and stories I am talking about. I have told all of them hundreds, if not thousands of times, and I study certain books over and over again. It's kind of like the Chess Grand Masters who study thousands of moves and arrangements of pieces until they can memorize a board without even looking at it. Oftentimes our expertise looks almost superhuman and inexplicable, but really we can develop certain skills through a commitment to consistent deliberate practice.

Mozart is one of my favorite examples of the talent myth. He didn't create his first masterpiece until he was 21 years old, and his father had started him on a deliberate practice regimen when he was 3 years old. EIGHTEEN YEARS of deliberate practice before he produced his first masterpiece! Was it talent, or tens of thousands of hours of deliberate practice?

Michelangelo said "If you knew what went into my mastery you wouldn't think it was so wonderful." Jerry Rice's workouts were so challenging that the guy who served as his strength coach wouldn't share them because he thought other people would get hurt if they tried them. He was always the first person at practice and the last to leave. Warren Buffett offered to work for free for his finance professor, but after doing a cost benefit analysis the professor turned Warren Buffett down. Walt Disney was fired from a local Kansas City newspaper for apparently "lacking creativity." Michael Jordan, possibly the greatest of all time, was cut from his high school team.

Another person many people don't know about is Swen Nater. Swen is the only person ever to be drafted in the first round of the NBA draft after never starting a game in college. Swen had an awesome dose of deliberate practice for four years at UCLA. His job everyday was to compete against the great Bill Walton. Swen is also the only person to have led the ABA and NBA in rebounding.

One side note for people who serve in coaching and teaching positions: **please remove the word *talent* from your vocabulary.** Carol Dweck's research on mindsets has shown that when you tell people they are talented or praise their results instead of effort, you push them towards the stifling "fixed mindset" and you can reinforce many of the very problems in those people you are frustrated with.

When researchers try to find talent it is very challenging, and they often come up empty when looking for early signs of it. Aside from some physical differences they can't really find talent, at least the talent most of us refer to when we use the word: a genetic predisposition to be great at something. **The picture that tends to emerge is always similar: the most skilled are the ones who have devoted the most time to deliberate practice. Which is why I always say.....**

The guy at the top of the mountain didn't fall there. Success always looks easy to those who weren't around while all the training happened. We may not all start with the same abilities, but where we start does not determine where we finish.

TRAIN To Be Clutch

- Read "Talent Is Overrated" by Geoff Colvin.
- Watch <u>"Success is not an accident"</u> video about Stephen Curry by @alanstein on the StrongerTeam *YouTube* channel.
- Study how Jack Delosa is building his empire in *Unprofessional*

CHAPTER

Where Does REAL Swagger Come From?

In one of my favorite movies, *Man on Fire*, Denzel Washington tells Dakota Fanning, "There are only two types of people in the world, trained and untrained. Which are you?"

Are you personally willing to guarantee you are trained, REGARDLESS of your circumstances?!

Can you walk into any environment, against any opponent, with pure confidence knowing you have done your very best to become the best you are capable of being?

Are you willing to do all the extra stuff? Are you willing to leave no stone unturned?
Can you do that?

And if you are willing to do it personally, are you willing to go to the next step? The next step is taking a teammate or a co-worker with you. It might be easy for you to get in the gym and get up shots by yourself, but the next level is bringing a teammate with you. You might be great at putting in the extra work to take the company to the next level, but are you mentoring the junior level executives, or just making them fend for themselves?

When Jamie had first come on board with our company, it wasn't good enough for me to just do things on my own. It was my responsibility to take him with me. It was my responsibility to give him opportunities to speak, to introduce himself, and to train people. Did this mean I was going to miss out on some opportunities? Yes, but it was better for US.

Sometimes **I** have to sacrifice for a better, longer term **WE**.

Here is the thing with pure confidence and real swagger: Lots of people talk about having swagger, "Ahhh Man! His swag is off the chain!" "She has mad-swagger!" Most of the time what they are referring to is what someone is wearing.

But REAL swagger can't be bought. It isn't what you wear or having the latest gear. Real swagger is pure confidence, and pure confidence only comes from having done the very best you are capable of doing to become the best you are capable of being. It comes from training. It comes from blood, sweat, and years of delayed gratification and deliberate practice to become the best you are capable of being.

I had the opportunity to be on a speaking ticket with Condoleeza Rice, and the day before I was speaking a woman who had been in coaching for a long time said to me, "Wow, I feel bad that you have to speak after Condoleeza Rice!" I laughed and said, "I have nothing but the utmost respect and admiration for Condoleeza Rice, but I believe the people in attendance will say I was a more dynamic and engaging speaker than her." Her mouth dropped a little bit, and she was in a bit of shock and awe that I would ever make such a statement. However, three months later she told that story before I worked with her program, and she said, "not only did he say that to me, but he went out and did exactly that."

Now, we are not promoting that you go around telling people you are the best in the world at what you do, but I know that I have done everything possible to become the very best that I am capable of being. Not only in the past, but I am currently studying and training every single day to continue to get better. Therefore, I believe I can walk into any environment and knock it out of the park. I can have that real swagger and pure confidence because I have trained to become the best speaker I can be.

So, my question for you is this....

Can you walk into any gym, any pitch meeting, any boardroom, onto any field, or whatever context you regularly find yourself in, with real swagger and pure confidence?

If you can't answer "yes" to that question, then what do you need to do to be able to have that real swagger? What do you need to start sacrificing to be able to have that level of confidence? You can have pure confidence; it isn't reserved for the chosen few. It will require ridiculous amounts of dedication, sacrifice, and training, but it is past possible!

Life Is Going To Punch You In The Face. What Are You Going To Do About It?

A guy goes to visit his friends in India and while they are at work he decides to visit an animal park. Now the zoo there is a little different than what he was used to back home. He was having a blast feeding all sorts of animals and interacting with them. But then he felt the ground start to shake. He turned around and his face turned from joy to terror! What he saw was a herd of elephants walking towards him. There was no fence or barrier between him and the beasts. All that was holding the elephants back was a little rope that was tied around their left hind legs, and a little Indian dude with a stick.

So he takes off running in the opposite direction until he finds someone who works at the zoo. He starts laying into this guy: "Are you guys crazy!?! Don't you know that those elephants are powerful beyond measure? They could snap that rope at any time and unleash their power knocking over everything in their wake!"

The zoo employee waits for the man to calm down and says, "I know that you're terrified and I know that the elephants are powerful beyond measure. But what you don't know is that when they are born, the very first thing we do is tie that rope around their leg. When they are young, the rope is actually stronger than them. It tells them what they can and can't do. It keeps them at bay and has control over them. As they grow older, they do so with the belief that the rope has power over them. Even though they have massive potential and are amazingly powerful, their belief about the rope holds them back."

The question we have to ask ourselves is:

What are those ropes in our lives that have been holding us back?

What are the beliefs that we are clinging to that are keeping us stuck?

What are the beliefs that may have been true at one point in our life, but that are no longer true and are keeping us from achieving our greatest potential?

One thing we like to say is, "Who says?"

Whenever someone says something is impossible, ask the question, "Who says?"

You aren't smart enough. "Who says?"

You need another degree to be successful in this economy. "Who says?"

You aren't tall enough. "Who says?"

You can never play for that team or in that league. "Who says?"

Look at Roger Banister. Before Roger Banister broke the four-minute mile, people everywhere believed it was impossible. Then after he broke it all of sudden people all over the world started running sub-four-minute miles. It wasn't a change in training habits. It wasn't that a new generation of runner was faster. The only thing that happened was the rope had been cut. A false belief had been shed and now people were free to tap into their greatest potential.

These false beliefs are all around us and many times we don't even know what they are until they are broken. People used to believe your skin color determined whether or not you had the intellectual acumen to play quarterback or lead a team. People used to believe your sex determined whether or not you could run a company or how much money you could make. People have believed all sorts of crazy things that have held us back from achieving our greatest potential. So, we must continually ask, "Who says?"

One of the most important things we need to decide is whether or not we believe our characteristics are carved in stone, or that they can be molded, shaped, and grow through deliberate practice. The former is what Stanford psychologist Carol Dweck calls a "fixed" mindset and the latter is the "growth" mindset.

We talk all the time about having a "growth" mindset, but I want to share a story with you about what it can practically look like under trying circumstances.

On New Year's Eve of 2012 I went down to San Diego to bring in 2013 with some of my friends from college. At the end of the night, all the venues at the Hard Rock Hotel let out at the same time and there were a lot of people who were all trying to get on the hotel elevators. Our group of fifteen or so people worked our way towards the elevator and half of our group got on the elevator while the other half of us did not.

All of sudden I heard someone say the most derogatory racist phrase you can say. It was so horrific; I couldn't believe it had been said. I must have been mistaken. Then I surveyed the crowd around me and there were only two African American people in the general vicinity, and both of them were my friends. Sure enough, one of them was pulling the other one away from where I thought I heard the person make the racist comment. So, I moved closer to where I thought it came from.

Sure enough, I heard the person say it again, "F&%* that N$&%&$!" and this time I was looking right at him. Now, I'm not sure exactly what I said, but it was probably something along these lines, "Are you FREAKING kidding me?!" I might have used a different word or two in the heat of the moment, but who can be sure?!

Apparently, he wasn't kidding.

Very quickly he jabbed me in the nose. Now, right as I was saying what I said to him I looked over his shoulder at the group of guys surrounding him. There were about four or five guys that would have made an NFL Defensive line look small. They had to have averaged 6'6" 270lbs.

I could have taken the first jab from the little guy. He was probably in the ballpark of 5'10" 155lbs, no big deal. But, while I was stunned from the quick first jab, one of the much larger guys throws a superman punch that knocked me out for plus or minus 15 seconds. Thankfully it was one of the smaller guys who threw the punch. He was only about 6'4" 240 lbs!!!

Even though I blacked out from the punch, I didn't actually get knocked off my feet. I like to tell people that's because I played division 1 athletics, but it was more likely because there were a lot of people around and I just pin-balled off of them.

As I came to, I was very confused at the liquid that was flowing all over my face like an ice cream cone on a hot summer day. When I saw a security guard with a shirt trying to stop the bleeding, I realized it was actually my blood everywhere.

A couple hours later after the bleeding stopped and I was able to take a shower, two of my friends took me to the hospital. As I am lying in the hospital bed I looked over at them and said, "I'm really glad that this happened! I believe it was in my best interest and an opportunity for me to learn and grow."

Imagine the looks on their faces and what was going through their mind. "Are you serious?! We knew you had a couple screws loose, but we brought you to the wrong hospital. That guy must have pushed you over the edge, you are officially crazy. How in the world could this be in your BEST interest?!"

But here is the thing: **LIFE IS GOING TO PUNCH YOU IN THE FACE!!!**

I sincerely hope it isn't a guy who is 6'4 240lbs, but life is going to punch you in the face. The job economy is the worst it has been in decades. Most college graduates can't get a job and are moving back in with their parents. Bad things happen in relationships. Over fifty percent of marriages are ending in divorce, and that's with fewer and fewer couples even making it to the altar. Infidelity is rampant in our culture. We are losing loved ones to cancer and other diseases.

Life is going to punch us in the face, and we *get to* decide whether we are going to have a victim mindset or a growth mindset.

We can believe there is nothing we can do and that we are just a victim of circumstance and just stay tied to that tree.

"My coach won't play me."

"No one will pay me what I'm worth."

"I'm not deserving of a healthy relationship."

"It doesn't matter what I do, it never works out."

OR

We can adopt a growth mindset and believe no matter what happens to me, it is in my best interest and an opportunity to learn and grow. We can ask, "What is one thing I can do to make this better?"

Which mindset are you going to adopt?

I will make you this promise: If you will adopt a growth mindset in every area of your life, you will become an unstoppable force.

How do you stop someone who has that growth mindset? How do you stop someone who can get knocked out by a guy who is 6'4" 240lbs, BUT who believes that is in their best interest and an opportunity to learn and grow?!

YOU CAN'T!

What is the alternative? To believe it is in your worst interest? All that does is put you in a victim mentality and all but guarantee that you will experience more of those things in the future.

Obviously, we don't want to get punched in the face, and if I could go backwards I would do things differently. BUT we can't go backwards in life! We can only move forward. So, the most beneficial thing we can do is adopt a growth mindset and believe everything that happens to us is in our best interest and an opportunity to learn and grow. We can't control what has happened, but we do have 100% control over the meaning we give the events in our lives.

You might be able to be successful, but you will never reach your potential without sacrifice, perseverance, and a growth mindset.

Remember! *You must have a growth mindset about having a growth mindset. It is going to take time and a lot of effort to adopt a growth mindset as your default mode of operation.*

TRAIN To Be Clutch

- Read Carol Dweck's *Mindset.*
- Then, read *Mindset* again! No, really. I'm serious.

What Do You Do When Your Building Doesn't Have A Trash Chute?

During undergrad we lived in a 6-story building with about a thousand other students. We paid upwards of $47,000 a year to attend this school and our dorm didn't even have a trash chute. We had to carry our trash onto the elevator, through the lobby, and about 200 yards to a dumpster down the road. Boohoo, I know! It sounds stupid, but it was pretty inconvenient.

After identifying the problem I settled on what I thought was a great solution: start a petition. So before practice one day I typed up a document in bold font saying something like: "We pay 47k$ a year to go to school here. Why don't we have a trash chute?!!!"

We went off to practice and I felt good having done something that I thought was revolutionary. As we returned from practice I was excited for the elevator doors to open and hopefully have a bunch of people incited to take action.

Instead of people supporting the cause, they tore my petition apart verbally.

Jamie says my face was priceless!

Things like, "Hey deutsche-bag, the dollar sign goes before the numbers not after them. You pay $47,000 and you can't even spell. Quit being a bit#% and carry out your own d$&! trash."

I have asked people in workshops if there was a more beneficial solution to my problem. Yet, never has anyone presented this solution. We aren't trained or equipped to actually create solutions to real world problems growing up, and this is why Jamie and I are so passionate about mentorship.

If I could go back in my life, I would say, "Joshua, you have a MASSIVE diamond in the rough opportunity. Rather, than try and incite your fellow classmates, START a trash collecting service. Charge $2-3 a week to collect people's trash and take it out for them. You can probably outsource the work, and take 20-30% off the top. AND you will have solved a real world problem!

Imagine walking into an interview and being asked "Can you please tell me a time when you took initiative and solved a problem?"

You tell them about the lack of a trash chute and the trash collecting service you started, BOOM, hired!

I have an intern who was telling me about the internship she was thinking about doing for the summer. She plays division 1 basketball and she needs a credit for her nutrition major. So she told me she was going to hand out snacks at a youth camp all summer.

Now, I know the experience could be an opportunity for growth in some regard. But by observing her body language and enthusiasm, and knowing what her ambitions are, I could tell that the experience would be less than ideal for helping her become the person she wants to become. So I said, "Ask me the question."

"What question?" she said.

I said, "Ok, I'll tell you the question to ask me because you have never been taught how to do this. Ask me 'Can you think of any other possibilities for an internship?'"

With a smile she asked me. "Okay," I said, "here are some ideas. You play basketball at the division-1 level and just wearing your school's sweat top gives you buy-in with many people.

What if you started your own organization?

You don't need a website, business model, t-shirts or banners. Just go out to one of the youth basketball clubs in your city and ask if you can serve. I guarantee that a parent will ask you to train her child. Do it and don't ask for money. Pour your life, knowledge, and heart into that child. I guarantee that if you do that, you will have 5-10 kids within a month that you can train. Don't do it for money, and I can almost guarantee you will get paid. Teach them about nutrition. Teach them what you have learned about the power of your mind. Teach them about basketball. Teach them about life."

Her eyebrows are continually rising!

"Now in the future when you are in interviews and they ask if you have provided a solution to a real-world problem, you can smile and explain. Not only that, you will have learned about serving people, loving people, and providing value. That is a mission-driven life. And knowing you, you will most likely change the lives of the kids you get to mentor."

Her jaw is dropping!

"Another option is interning with a skills trainer." "How would I do that?" she asked.
"Great question! Now you're learning! It just so happens that I have a good friend who runs one of the premier basketball skills academies in the country, and he was telling me that he needs some help. He loves Jesus, will train you, will mentor you, and will

help you grow as a person and in your sport. I can ask him the question."

Now she is grinning ear to ear!

"Or if you want to go overseas I can get you in touch with the missions organization I worked with and you can serve in Ireland, train, and provide value out there."

Now she is shaking her head!

"I want you to know this isn't because of *who* you know. These ideas are coming because you asked a few good questions from somebody who might know a bit more than you. And because of your hustle and your track record with that person, he is willing to help in any way possible. When you are faithful with little, you will be made faithful with much."

Jamie and I have been blown away by the opportunities and results that have manifested when we committed to learning to ask better questions from great mentors. It takes a lot of vulnerability to ask someone for help. It's one way of stripping back the fear of what other people think about us. But more than that, it opens the door for real and meaningful relationships and an expansion on what we perceive to be possible.

Do you want to experience more than you ever thought was possible?
Seek out quality mentors and learn to ask better questions.

TRAIN To Be Clutch

- Read *Power Questions.*
- Who could you ask to serve as a mentor to you?
- Who can you study that will provide insight into how they have grown?

- Who do you follow on social media? Are they providing value? Most of the people who do awesome stuff are giving out their wisdom for free or minimal cost on twitter. Again I ask, who are you following?

CHAPTER

Apply It Before You Preach It

"Are you going to tell your son to chase his dreams? If so, then you better have chased yours."

You ever had someone say something that just pierced you to the core? Joshua Michael Medcalf did that with those very words in the summer of 2012.

Amy and I had just returned from Ireland and were settling in Denver while we were expecting our first child. It had long been my dream to play soccer at the highest level possible. It was one of those dreams that I felt God had placed there. The thing was I had just come back from Ireland where I had a pelvis injury that kept me from playing soccer for nearly two years. I had seen every specialist and had numerous scans, but there had been no healing.

Within the first four weeks of being back I found a chiropractor who was phenomenal and through her and her family's help and a lot of prayer, I was healed. "But," I was telling myself, "you haven't played for two years and you are getting a bit older." This was back when I knew nothing about talking to myself rather than just listening. And this was right before Joshua started working with me on the mental side of life.

I went out to visit Joshua in LA and during that time I shared with him this crazy dream that made no sense. That was when he shared those words with me. Within a few months I decided to knock on all the doors possible and when that didn't work out, I showed up to the Colorado Rapids' training ground, waited until practice was over, shook one of the staff members' hand and asked if I could play.

It sounds sooooo foolish looking back and I felt like such an idiot and loser during that time. But two days later I began the hardest period of my life mentally, physically, and spiritually as I trained with the team for the remaining five months of the season.

I chased my dream. It was a dream, not a goal. We can talk about that another time.

In his book, *Transforming Prayer*, Daniel Henderson shares one of my favorite stories. There is a dad who is sitting in his chair reading the newspaper after a meal. His young son was continually asking him to come play on the floor but the dad just tried to give him something else to be occupied with. After a bit of persistence, the dad ripped out a page of the paper that had a picture of the whole world. He tore the picture up into small pieces and said, "When you put this map of the world back together, we will go out and play."

He continued his reading thinking that his son would be engaged in the map for quite some time. But only a few minutes later his son returned with the map taped back together. The dad couldn't believe that he did it so quickly and thought he must be a genius in geography. So he asked his son how he did it so quickly. His son replied, "It was easy. There is a picture of a man on the back. When I got the man right, I got the world right too." I wonder what would happen if we focused first on applying things to ourselves, rather than pointing out how other people need to change?

During my time training people across the country I've heard many people in leadership roles vent about how the people on their team are just not willing to take things seriously. They are not willing to sacrifice. They don't know what is possible. But often, it's the very same people who are not willing to commit to reading, training their physiology, finding new strategies, altering their language, and writing out their cue cards daily. *Maybe it is time we take a hard look in the mirror.*

If we want people to follow us and strive towards reaching their greatest potential, then we better be modeling that daily. Jesus didn't just talk; he walked. He put his life on the line. He put his reputation on the line. He gave up what he could have had to invest in what he believed truly mattered.

I asked a person in coaching the other day to please let the people on his team see some hustle in his own life if he really wanted them to be motivated. His response: "I already did the grinding when I played in college. It's their turn."

It's taken me a while to get here, but I do not talk about things that I am not currently doing myself. When I ask people to analyze how they use their time, I make sure that I paint the rainbow on my ICal as well. When I talk to people about seeking training that is just outside of their comfort zone, I find workouts that literally make me sick just thinking about them. When I tell people to pursue those God-ordained passions and desires, I write and pray most days circling things in prayer that in my mind terrify the life out of me and sound down-right foolish.

Am I perfect? No. Am I getting better? Yes. That's all I'm asking people to do. Right now I am chasing dreams that make no sense given where I am at. I am trying daily to put first things first instead of going out and spending money on things I want. I am working on becoming the type of person that I wrote I wanted to be when I configured my obituary.

I know that there are a lot of "I" statements in here, but with everything we do, it has to start internally with you. If we are serious about the type of influence we want to have in this world, let's take a serious look at how we use our time, spend our money, talk to ourselves, and what we habitually do.

TRAIN To Be Clutch

- Some of us can start small while others can immerse themselves in this. Give yourself grace. Choose a growth mindset as you try to have a growth mindset. Know that your worth does not come from what you do, but from who and whose you are. Embrace the path to mastery knowing that it will be hard.
- Each day focus on getting a little bit better, a littler bit better, a little bit better.
- Be deliberate. Be consistent. Be the change you want to see in the world.

Change More Lives By Being Selfish

One of the most enjoyable exercises we get to do in workshops is having people evaluate their self-talk. To do this I have them go back to a big mistake they have made in the recent past. It could have been on the field in practice, during a game, in the office, or even trying to talk to a girl they liked. I have them relive the moment and try to remember what they said to themselves right after. Then I have them turn to the person to their right and with the same words, vigor, intensity and heart posture say to that person what they said to themselves.

Go ahead and try it yourself! What usually happens is that 2% of those people actually yell it out laughingly, 28% whisper it to their neighbor, and 70% sit quietly with the most horrified and paralyzed look on their face you've ever seen. Clearly through the laughs and nervous tension, the point is made: We would never say to others what we say to ourselves. "Why?" I ask. "Because it's mean, hurtful, and isn't going to help that person get better," they say.

Interesting isn't it? **We are not willing, the majority of the time, to tear someone else down but we have no problem thrashing ourselves to bits!** Jesus was asked about the greatest commandment and he said there are two:

"Love the Lord your God with all your heart, mind, soul and strength. And the second is like it: love others as yourself."

I always ask people, "Who are we called to love?" Most say God and others. But really there are three people we are to love. Love God, love others, *in the same way as you* love yourself. Let's be honest, if we loved others the way we love ourselves then things would look pretty dismal given the results from the exercise above.

We can try to be an excellent teammate, friend, or leader to those around us, but are we really giving them our best if this is how we coach ourselves? When training to serve as a lifeguard, you are taught that when swimming out to rescue someone in the ocean, you are the number one concern. Though that sounds selfish, it's more selfless and helpful than you think. When retrieving someone from a spot where there are solid obstacles such as rocks or poles suspending a pier, you are instructed to place the person you are saving between you and the object. That way if the waves push you into the rocks, you don't risk injury or worse because, let's be honest, how effective are you as a lifeguard if you can't move your arms or are unconscious? The same goes for flying on a plane. When I have my one year-old on my lap, it goes against every moral fiber in my body, but I am supposed to put on my oxygen mask before assisting my son!

One of the hardest things for many people to do is soak up the good things that others say to us or about us. I was dropping my son off at camp one day and the leader told me that she loves seeing my wife everyday. Just her presence makes the place a different environment. What a wonderful thing to say! So I told Amy this one-day and she just looked down and said, "That's sweet." So I grabbed her by both shoulders, looked deep into her in the eyes and said, "NO! Either you soak it up or continue to treat yourself poorly!" The correct response is "Thank You!" (This was all done in love and we are still lovingly married!)

We have this false humility that is prevalent in our culture where we suppress the wonderful things that people say to us. The flip side is that we often ruminate on and amplify the negative things people say about us! I had a guy say to me after a game recently that I have the quickest feet he has ever seen. Now, I can explain that away by saying, "This guy is old, short, and plays in the coed recreational league. Of course I have the quickest feet *he* has ever seen." Or I can soak it up and amplify it. I dwell on it so that it sows a wonderful belief into my heart and starts to shape the way I view myself as I train and play.

I have gone back in my memory to find some crucial moments in my life where someone said something to me that meant a lot and gave me a boost in confidence. Knowing that such compliments are few and far between. One of the girls I train asked me, "Well if I do that, then I feel like I will be cocky or arrogant." But here is the thing:

Arrogance = Better Than
Confidence = Getting Better

People in leadership can most likely agree that one of the biggest frustrations is that others don't believe in themselves the way we believe in them. But remember, when we point the finger at others, there are always three fingers pointing back. If we want others to build their own confidence, we must be willing to do the same.

So really, in order to be extremely effective, uphold the great commandment, and to make strides towards our fullest potential, we need to love *ourselves* first. Call it selfish, call it arrogant, but call it what it is: essential! Being intentional about developing beneficial and constructive self-talk is absolutely fundamental in loving ourselves and becoming excellent at business, leadership, sports, and friendship!

God not only created you, but He loves you so much He sent His only Son to die for you. Talking to yourself in very negative ways is kind of slapping Him in the face.

TRAIN To Be Clutch

- Would you hang out with people who talk to you the way you talk to yourself?
- Are you very intentional about how you talk to yourself, especially in highly emotional moments?
- We are constantly preaching a sermon to ourselves every single day, and most of us need to preach a new sermon. The self-condemning, horrible negative and destructive track isn't helping us get any better.
- Grab a 4x6 notecard and write out some beneficial and constructive self-talk statements you can say to yourself after you make a mistake. For the people we train who love Jesus, we ask them to write out what Jesus would say to them. Remember, every encounter Jesus had with the misfits, the outcasts, the downtrodden, and the most deformed and messed up members of society he spoke to them with undeserved love, compassion, and relentless grace.
- Here are some examples of beneficial and constructive self-talk statements:
    - -Next play.
    - -The next opportunity I will _____.
    - -Breathe, and get the next one.
    - -Play present.
    - -Relax, keep your head down, and make a solid swing.
    - -Fake a pass to make a pass.
    - -Bring the action.
    - -I got this.
    - -I can do this.
    - -Focus.
    - -My value comes from who I am, not what I do.
    - -Enjoy the tough stuff, because you are going to miss it later.
    - -Fall in love with the process of becoming great.
    - -I am on the path to mastery.

-The tough stuff brings out the best in me.

-This is in my best interest.

-What an amazing opportunity to learn and grow.

• Remember:

WORDS *put pictures in our mind.*

Pictures in our mind impact how we feel.

How we feel impacts what we do.

What we habitually do impacts our worldly destiny.

How God REALLY Feels About You (you might be surprised what it says....)

I don't expect you to believe what I believe, but this is what I believe. I hope it encourages you.

You are His child who He loves a billion times more than anything you could ever imagine. He fearfully and wonderfully made you. He knit you in your mother's womb. He paid His life for you to have peace that flows like a waterfall over your heart, and the joy of a kid at Disneyland. He didn't just die to get you into heaven. He died to get heaven into you. His love endures forever.

Your true identity doesn't come from what you do, but whose you are. If you live by your feelings, you will be destroyed by them. The price heaven paid for you determined your value. Therefore, you are the most valuable thing on earth, because God sacrificed His son for you. A life for a life. Live from the finished work of Jesus. If you live from this point you are free from living out of the judgment and opinions of this world. You are His most treasured jewel, worth more than anything on this earth. You are His most prized possession. Do not be conformed to this world, but be transformed by the renewing of your mind.

Too often we are seeking counsel instead of the Counselor. Love never fails, so you can never be rejected because His love for you is perfect. Seek His kingdom first, it crushes everything. God made us righteous with undeserved kindness through faith in Jesus. Where we come out of doesn't determine where we finish. Jesus' finished work determines who we are and where we finish. God said "Yes" to us, so it doesn't matter who says "No." Your fact doesn't change His truth. Let Jesus speak louder to you than anything in this world, including your current circumstances. When things are going well, trust in Jesus. When things are going horrible, trust in Jesus. When things are just going, trust in Jesus. When you don't know what else to do, trust in Jesus. He will give you deep and fulfilling rest and peace. He loves you, because He loves you, because He loves you, because He loves you, because He loves you, because He loves you.

Jesus is passionately pursuing your heart, not behavior modification. The crux of Christianity is not what I do for God, but what God did for us.

Religion = DO. Jesus = DONE.

He lived the life we should have lived, and He died the death we should have died.

The most powerful force in the universe is pleased and loves you, so you are free to conquer the world. Perfect love casts out fear, and His love for you is perfect. He wants you to have perpetual rest and never to worry about anything.

If you want to know who God is, all you have to do is look at Jesus, because He represents the character of God. Every encounter Jesus had with misfits, thieves, adulterers, the broken, the dead, the dying, the sick, the downtrodden, and the most outcast members of society, He healed them, restored them, and loved them passionately, undeservedly, and unconditionally.

God showed His GREAT love for us by sending Jesus to die for us while we were absolutely useless to Him and did nothing to deserve it. His power works best in our weakness.

You didn't get into God's family because of your performance, and you won't get kicked out because of your performance. God chose to love you because of who He is, not because of who you are or what you did. Therefore, He's not going to stop loving you. Do everything from the deep satisfaction of knowing that God passionately, relentlessly, indescribably, lavishly, and unconditionally loves you.

Fix your thoughts and focus on what is true, honorable, right, pure, lovely, and admirable. Think about things that are excellent and worthy of praise. Count it joy when you experience trials, because they will strengthen your faith. Be content in every circumstance. Live with unconditional gratitude.

I pray that your love will overflow more and more, and that you will keep on growing in knowledge and understanding. I pray you would come to know who He REALLY is, and who that makes you. I pray that the peace that passes all understanding would guard your heart and mind in Christ Jesus. I pray Jesus would break every chain in your life. I pray His truth and love will pierce your heart and transform your mind.

If you want to learn more about how God really feels about you, I suggest you download the "Jesus Is" Music Project on iTunes or listen to some talks from Judah Smith at http://thecity.org/index. php/media

A Better Way To Becoming More Than We Ever Dreamed Possible

I wonder what a team would look like if they only focused on growth? What if the people coaching only spoke to the people on their team about getting better that day in practice or during a game? Is that doable? Is that sustainable? Is that even an option?

Well the majority of information in our society flies in the face of this idea, but it's exactly what happened to the Butler Men's Basketball program when Brad Stevens took over in the head coaching position. He and his staff took a group of people most top program's didn't even recruit, to back-to-back national championship games.

In his current position holding the most historic coaching job in NBA history, Stevens had this to say about goals: *"I know it sounds strange, but I don't really have goals. I focus on getting better every single day."*

Did you catch what he said: *Focus on getting better!* Is it really that simple? Surely he talks about how many games they want to win to make it to the playoffs. Surely as a Christian he must quote the apostle Paul who said he presses on towards the *goal* of his faith.

Surely he tells his team how important the upcoming game is to their record. Not that we know of. We don't know every word that comes out of his mouth but we do know that every time someone interviews and asks him about his goals, he tells them, "I know it sounds strange, but I don't really have goals. I just focus on getting better every day."

Focus on growth!

Let go of outcome-based thinking.

Focus on doing the very best you can, right where you are, using what you have, and do all three things steadily and consistently overtime.

Do *this and* you will most likely wake up one day and find that you have accomplished amazing things, BUT more importantly, you will be amazed at the personal characteristics you have refined and who you have become as a person in the process.

Focusing on growth is *sustainable*. One of the most frustrating things in sports, business and relationships, however, is that people often base their efforts on results. The further their goal is from being achieved, the less passion and resolve they have to show up early to practice for extra shots. When the bonuses stop coming in, the extra effort for the client tends to fade. As external results and outcome-based praise grow further from view, most often our process tanks. Instead of dwelling on what we do have and what we can do and growth every day, when we are goal-focused our minds are bombarded by what we don't have and what we cannot control.

This is the epitome of the *victim mentality*. This is the state of thought and life where we feel like the people refereeing, the economy, our significant others, the people coaching, our colleagues, bosses, resources, location, weather, and background are colluding and conspiring against us. Rather than choosing to focus all our energy on the things under our control and using our circumstances as an opportunity to develop true mental toughness, we choose to dwell on the uncontrollable variables and circumstances that leave us feeling like victims in life.

The crazy thing is that the principle works the other way too! How often do we hear bosses refusing to praise considerable growth for fear of complacency? We cannot tell you how many people coaching struggle to acknowledge their people's growth for fear that they will believe they have *arrived* and have nothing more to improve upon. A problem with goals is that oftentimes they actually increase the likelihood of skimping out on the process. When we focus on the goals we dwell on the outcome instead of the refining process of the journey. In this state, it is nearly impossible to give adequate attention to the process of growth—the very thing that influences results!

Focus on progress and achievement will take care of itself.

We had the pleasure of working with a person who loved the people on his team dearly, but who had focused on winning his whole career. The only thing was his team hadn't won a tournament in half a decade. They were always highly ranked, but could never actually win. We came in and had them burn their goals, focus on growth, focus on the process, focus on true mental toughness, and put first things first.

They won their next two out of three tournaments and almost won the national title.

Apparently the "Kool-Aid" is worth drinking. ☺

Those Destined For Greatness Must First Walk Alone In The Desert

Those destined for greatness must
first walk alone in the desert.

-Winston Churchill

We live in a culture obsessed by achievement. The bright lights of television have left many of us with the obsession of "making it." However, I think in the era of steroids, cheating scandals, Enron, and "instant" everything, we have lost an appreciation for the desert. According to studies done by Harvard, the greatest predictor of future success is the ability to delay gratification. Put another way, the greatest predictor of future success is the ability to traverse the desert.

The desert is where you have to battle the demons in your head telling you that you will never make it, you are a fraud, and everyone is going to find out.

The desert is where it seems everyone is telling you to give up your dreams. The desert is where your failures are all anyone wants to talk about. The desert is where it seems you are crazy for pursuing the dream planted deep inside your heart.

The desert is where you learn to fall in love with the journey, not the results. The desert is where you learn that failure is a learning tool, and an inescapable part of becoming who you are destined to be. The desert is where you learn the greatest lessons come from failure, not success. The desert is where you learn to fall in love with the process of becoming great.

The desert is where a lot of people turn their backs on you. The desert is where your true character is not only tested, but it is refined.

The desert is where we learn to put first things first. The desert is where we learn that people are so much more important than achievement. The desert is where we learn to trust in God more than people.

No one can escape the desert. Some might be required to spend more time there than others, but much like "the path to mastery" it applies to everyone, and is unavoidable.

Even Jesus didn't avoid the desert. Before He stepped into His public ministry He went to the desert and was tempted by the Devil while fasting for 40 days.

Derrick Coleman won a Super Bowl with the Seahawks this year, but not after going un-drafted and almost no one believing he could play in the NFL being deaf. In many ways, he is always in his desert.

Michael Jordan went to his desert after being cut from his high school team.

Peyton Manning went to his desert as he was overcoming two neck surgeries and having to learn a completely new way to throw a football.

Steve Jobs went to his desert for more than 10 years after being fired from Apple, until they finally begged him to come back and save the company he created.

Walt Disney went to his desert after being fired from a local Kansas City newspaper and told he lacked creativity.

I went through my desert after Duke, when I moved to LA and lived in a homeless shelter for 6 months, then the closet of a gym for 9 months, and then cut out almost everything in my life for another 6-9 months to study and read like a med-student.

Some think you become great on the big stage under the bright lights, but the bright lights only reveal our work in the desert. Churchill was right, "those destined for greatness must first walk alone in the desert." Embrace your desert, rather than run from it. Most will avoid it at all costs, but the few who embrace it will step into their greatness and change the world.

We NEED To Struggle and Fight

In every area of life it seems to me that having less initial resources, success, and opportunity are actually the building blocks of sustained greatness.

Most people will not thrive under these conditions, but the ones with a stubborn persistence, and willingness to creatively experiment despite circumstances, are the ones who go on to reach the pinnacles of greatness in the world.

It is through their lack of physical resources that they are stretched to levels of intellectual creativity and resourcefulness others have never been forced to tap into. Much like a mother finding the strength to lift a car off her child, they find inner strength, persistence, and resourcefulness that only extreme circumstances can bring out.

We talk about it and we "know" that:

- Apple started in a garage
- Facebook in a dorm room
- Jordan was cut from his high school team

- The founder of IKEA had to ride his bike three hours into Stockholm as a 12 year old to buy matchsticks in bulk
- Walt Disney was fired from a newspaper for lacking creativity and that his first movie sucked according to critics
- Oprah was fired for not being fit/pretty enough for TV
- *Unbroken* was a true story
- Victor Frankl wrote "Man's search for meaning" after losing his family and suffering through Nazi concentration camps
- *Boeing's* first plane was awful and that they had to make furniture to keep the business afloat
- *3m* (makers of post it notes) persistently failed along life for their first 11 years and during that time the CEO never couldn't even draw a salary
- Sony struggled so bad in the beginning they were selling make-shift heating pads just to survive

The examples are endless....

There is something about experiencing repeated failure and lack of resources, that is a part of the formula for bringing out the deepest creativity, resourcefulness, and persistence needed to reach one's personal greatness.

We know these stories, but how often do we create these environments?

How often do we create the exact opposite environment?

We see that kids with almost negligible resources and opportunities in developing countries are markedly more joyful than people in the United States.

And everyday we hear or see another person who has been given every resource and opportunity to become great (and most are very, very good) at their craft, quit, and claim they are miserable and don't want to do it anymore.

It's like somewhere fundamentally wired into our DNA we need to struggle and fight. We need to be presented with massive challenges and be given the opportunity to overcome them.

Maybe those who are given everything on a silver platter feel like they are cheating, and slowly it erodes them at their core.

I think our desire to make things easier and give those we lead, whether they are our sons and daughters, employees, or members of our team, resources and experiences we never had might actually be crippling their chances of becoming truly great and reaching their fullest potential.

Our efforts might give them a better chance of not failing as hard, but it's giving them an even greater chance of being highly mediocre at everything they touch in comparison to their ultimate potential.

Ironically, and counter-culturally, we might be better off trying to make things more challenging than less challenging. Maybe we should be creating intentional constraints on resources instead of giving those we lead all the resources needed to be "successful".

Because that "success" and those resources might be the greatest obstacle to them becoming everything they can be. *Maybe they get a "good" job, and have a white picket fence with a dog and two kids, but what if they had the potential to find a cure for cancer or start the next Apple, but you gave them what they wanted instead of what they needed?*

Our fear of failure for the next generation is creating people primed for mediocrity at best and crippled at worst in comparison to their greatest potential. Sadly, in an era of never before seen opportunity and resources, a generation of people are unprepared to seize almost any of it.

Excellence Sells Itself

You don't ever see commercials for certain products. You don't ever see "Buy 2 get 1 free sale" at Louis Vuitton. You don't ever see anyone trying to get you into a Ferrari store on television.

Everyday people walk into those stores with their checkbook in hand ready to pay top dollar for their products.

Why don't they have to have sales and commercials? Because greatness never goes on sale and excellence sells itself!

If you commit to mental training and applying the principles in this book consistently and carefully over time in your life, you won't have to worry about trying to sell yourself any more. *Excellence sells itself.* Your track record will start to speak for you. People will start knocking on your door and you will start having to turn down opportunities.

You have to offer discounts and do all sorts of fancy marketing if you have an inferior product, but excellence sells itself.

In closing......

On your deathbed you won't wish you won more, made more money, or acquired more stuff. You will wish you developed deeper relationships and loved people more. I learned as a 9 year old when I pulled my best friend and little brother out of our pool that life is fragile and very short. Sometimes people wonder why we do what we do, and it probably somehow ties back to that. We try and love people deeply because we know they can be gone tomorrow.

When we put first things first, second things are not suppressed but they actually increase. Your value comes from who you are, and not what you do. You are a child of God who happens to play a sport, coach, run a business, or whatever it is that you do. Don't let your identity be defined by what you do; it is a recipe for disaster. Cultivate unconditional gratitude every day. Visualize yourself performing at your best, but also visualize yourself overcoming the inevitable challenges and adversity that come in sports and life.

Become your own best friend by practicing CONSTRUCTIVE and BENEFICIAL self-talk. Make sure you are the rock of Gibraltar with your body language for your team and your family. Make a commitment to a NO EXCUSES life. Take responsibility; never blame anyone, including yourself. Make sure what you do with your 86,400 seconds every day and your willingness to sacrifice are in direct proportion to the size of your dreams. Burn your goals. Focus on the vision for your life. Fall in love with the process and the journey. Let the results take care of themselves.

Develop true mental toughness by having a great attitude, giving your very very best, treating people really really well, and having unconditional gratitude regardless of your circumstances. Use your current context as a vehicle. Please don't be another person who gets used by their sport, business, or job. Commit to living by your principles rather than your feelings.

Comparison is the thief of all joy. Do the best you can, with what you have, right where you are at. Remember, the person at the top of the mountain didn't fall there. Greatness always looks easy to those who weren't around when all the training is going on.

People who do average work are convinced there are shortcuts to becoming great, but there is only blood, sweat, and years of delayed gratification and deliberate practice. Either pay the price of regret or the price to become great. Dream Bigger. Think smaller. Be faithful with all the small stuff in your hand right now. Love more. Judge less. Serve more. Provide value. Focus on training to become the best you are capable of being, and become the change you wish to see in the world.

One day you just might wake up and realize your real life is better than your dreams.

More resources, Bonus Material and a Sneak Peak:

Our focus at T2BC is transformed hearts and transformed minds through love and mentorship. We have a few different ways that we tackle this mission. First, we try and provide as much value as possible through t2bc.com and twitter:

@jdgilbert19 & @joshuamedcalf

We also offer:
- Online Training Programs
- Team Workshops
- Keynote Speaking
- Mentorship Programs
- 90 Day Training Manuals
- Corporate Retreats

If you would like to find out more visit us at t2bc.com or contact Jamie@traintobeclutch.com or Joshua@traintobeclutch.com

SNEAK PEAK

"An Impractical Guide To Becoming A Transformational Leader"

-CHAPTER 1-

YOU Matter

You don't need to spend too much time around me before I bring up Judah Smith. In my opinion he is the best in the world at sharing stories in public speaking, hands down.

Another one of my friends who does a lot of public speaking and is world renowned at his craft said, "Judah is the best, and no one else is even close."

I agree.

I've only spent about 5 minutes with Judah in a private setting and I chose my questions carefully. The first question I asked him was, "What do you know now that you wish you would have known when you first started out?"

Every week I study Judah's work. I listen to his mp3's. I've read his books. I listen to him live twice a week even though he gives the same talk twice, I take notes and stay for both. His thinking, writing, and speaking have *greatly* influenced all of mine. However, nothing has hit me as hard as his response to that question.

He said, "When I started out, I tried to write the BEST sermons. Now I just try and love the people in the audience."

When I started out, I tried to be the best in the world at performance psychology. My focus was teaching mental training exercises, tips, and tricks to increase performance.

Today, I start almost every talk with "YOU Matter."

I let people know that they matter.
Not what they do.
Not what they achieve.
Not their goals.
Not their stuff.
Not their accomplishments.
Not their dreams.
THEY matter.
YOU matter.
You are a human BEING, not just a human DOING.

I probably would have laughed at someone if they had tried to explain this to me 5 years ago. Now it is the most important part of what we do at Train To Be CLUTCH. We used to focus on performance enhancement, now we focus on helping people know and feel that they are loved unconditionally for who they ARE, not what they DO.

What you learn in this book, if applied consistently and carefully over time, can help you tap into your greatest potential as a person who leads people. BUT until you experience a true heart posture shift and value human beings for who they are, you will remain trapped in transactional leadership.

People can feel and know in their heart whether you really care about them, or if it is just a strategy. *It can't just be a strategy*.

I can't trust you to love me if you don't love yourself.

We can't give something we don't have.
We have to accept unconditional love before we can give it.

The challenge I've seen is that many people in leadership had parental figures who showed love sparingly, and the parents only showed up and gave love, attention, and affection when they *ACHIEVED* something.

This pattern created achievement addicts.
This pattern created approval addicts.

Underneath it all is a desperate need for approval and achievement, because deep down we think *that* is what makes us loveable. We think we aren't loveable without the doing and achieving.

But deep down we are all seeking authentic and deep unconditional love. We are tired of the performance.

Our HEART is tired.
Our SOUL is tired.

We can break the cycle.
You can break the cycle.

In order to break the cycle at a foundational level, you must understand that your value comes from who you are.

If you don't love yourself, how can you be trusted to love those you lead?

You will always have a tendency to operate out of fear instead of love.

Fear of losing their love.
Fear of losing your job.
Fear of losing your respect.
Fear of always having to prove something.

If you are looking to an outside source for worth, approval, and love, you will always operate out of the fear of losing it.

God already unconditionally loves you, and His steadfast love endures forever. It has never been about your performance, and it never will be about your performance. Therefore, you are free to accept His love, love yourself, and finally be freed to love others with no strings attached.

Who you become forever and always trumps what you achieve.

Transformational leaders have nothing to prove, only love to give.

Perfect love casts out fear.

We do not expect you to believe everything that we believe, and even if you don't believe what we believe, we think you can find immense value from the stories, tools, and strategies within. Our hope is that you will feel encouraged, refreshed, and maybe even a little bit lighter after reading this book.
Let our journey begin!

-*CHAPTER*-

Transformational vs. Transactional

Memories of transactional leaders can haunt people for a lifetime.

Maybe it was a person who was your coach.
Maybe it was a person who was your pastor.
Maybe it was a person who was your teacher.
Maybe it was a person who was your boss.

Transactional leadership always makes people feel like production units.

I was sitting at a lunch with a lot of people who give money to support a certain BCS school's program when I heard the man responsible for leading the baseball program say, "Well, you have to remember that we have over 700 innings walking out the door next year." He was referring to the young men he had the responsibility of leading, but that little reference was a picture of his heart posture. They were production units first, not human beings.

"From the abundance of the heart the mouth speaks." Luke 6:34

Many people tell me they felt more pressure from shooting or kicking a ball in little league, high school, or collegiate sports than they did later in life in what could be considered much more stressful situations.

In leadership:

What you say matters.
What you do matters.
HOW you do it matters even more.

Those things will likely be remembered for a lifetime by those you lead, and those leadership patterns also have a high likelihood of being passed down for generations.

You have a responsibility and opportunity to encourage, bring hope, and inspire. But too often this opportunity is soiled and the modus operandi in leadership is to take the easy way out and demean, criticize, and use people.

It is easy to get caught up in the moment and lose perspective. It is easy to believe that winning is what really matters, and it is SO EASY to justify.

If we don't win I can't provide for my family.
If I don't get this contract I will lose my job.
If I don't turn these numbers around I will be fired.

It's easy to find fault, criticize, and blame.
It's hard to take responsibility, have patience, and encourage.

Transformational leadership is the toughest, but most rewarding path you can embark on. It takes time and almost impossible patience. It is requires authentic vulnerability, linguistic intentionality, and a willingness to do the dirty work no one likes to do. It requires putting first things first, and people above profits and winning. Transformational leadership builds authentic relationships based on love, and helps build people into becoming everything they are capable of becoming.

Transformational leadership isn't soft; rather, it is a different kind of strength not easily recognized. It is the type of strength exhibited by people who can get struck in the cheek and have the courage not to fight back, even though they could. It is the strength of someone like Gandhi and MLK's non-violent resistance. It is the type of strength it takes for a kid in middle school to go over and sit with the person sitting by themselves at lunch.

Transactional leadership is shallow, sometimes quick, but lacks the depth of foundation needed to transform lives. It puts profits and winning above relationships, and it leaves a wake of emotional baggage and broken hearts. Transactional leaders push people toward performance-based identity prisons and the emotional roller coaster of finding your self-worth in achievement. Transactional leadership builds relationships to find trigger points to manipulate people to get results.

For many years I operated as a transactional leader, and I left a lot of hurting people in my wake.

The good news is that it is never too late to invest in yourself and make changes. Believing we can change is more than half the battle. If you want to become a transformational leader, you have to become a better you.

Both of us, as the authors of this book, have learned how to become transformational leaders; None of us were born with it, and all of us slip up at times, myself probably more than Jamie.

We have the privilege of mentoring and speaking into the lives of people all over the world from many different backgrounds and passions. Some of them are world class at what they do, and the others are just beginning their journey. The thing that is consistent is that we get to see people learn, grow, and change for the better every single day.

The truth is, everyone is a mentor; it just takes some people longer to realize their role than others. I love what Joe Ehrmann says about mentorship in his book, *Inside Out Coaching*:

"Imagine if coaches (leaders) today thought of themselves as mentors or aspired to the ideals of mentoring: I am the head mentor or I'm the mentor of the defensive line. Think how much that might have changed the coach-player relationship—a title conveying an *UNDENIABLE OBLIGATION* to care for players' welfare, instruct them in virtue, and guide them toward an adulthood of citizenship and contemplation."

When I speak I operate under the assumption that at least one or two of the people in the room are actively considering taking their own life. We know a guy who coaches that had a person who played for him take her own life, and it changed his perspective on leadership forever. I want to lead and mentor as if hearts and lives are on the line, because I believe they truly are.

Would you operate differently if someone you were responsible for leading took their own life? Really think about that. Would winning or profits seem so important if that happened? Too often manipulation is being disguised and justified as love, but those we lead aren't fooled and this only exasperates their pain.

Too often I meet adults who still have scars that have never healed from transactional leadership that hurt and used them. You have probably had a similar experience with someone in leadership at some point in your life as well. It is disgusting and disdainful. Sometimes those people have done awful things and abused their power physically, but other times they have done significant damage emotionally without ever inappropriately touching a person.

Our world needs an influx of people committed to transformational leadership. We are honored and grateful for the opportunity to shed some light on how to become a transformational leader.

Becoming transformational is not practical, it's not easy, but it is transformational.

Please remember, most books like these are authors writing advice to themselves, and this book is no exception ☺

-CHAPTER-

Is That Really *Your* Dream?

If there is one thing that drives me up the wall, it is someone I just met asking me "What do you do?"

I have come up with a myriad of responses to that question:
- "Are you asking what I do to make money and provide for my family?"
- "I do a lot of things. I like to write, sing, play golf, etc..."
- "I serve as a professional story teller."
- "I get to mentor people in all walks of life."
- "I am uncomfortable with that question."
- "The sky is blue." (Joshua's personal favorite.)

Inevitably there is 30-foot stretch of path at my home golf course between the 1st green and the 2nd tee where this question perpetually seems to be asked.

One day I was playing with a younger guy who plays competitive golf and we reached this stretch of path. Trying to redeem that ground, I asked what I think is a better question:

"Sam, what is your dream?"

Without hesitation, he replied, "I want to play on the PGA Tour!"

I took a few seconds, smiled at him, and then asked one of the best questions I've ever asked:

"Is that really *your* dream, or is that just how you define success in your sport?"

I get to ask people a lot of questions, and I have never seen someone so puzzled and dumbfounded. He tried to talk, but every time he opened his mouth he just paused and went deep into thought.

Maybe it was his dream, or maybe it was just the dream that was conditioned in his mind.

As I work with people across sport and business I am astounded at how many people *say* they want to operate at the highest level of their sport or industry, but later reveal that they truly want something else. It's as if there is shame in not wanting to play professionally.

If you do want to play at the highest level, great!
If you do want to operate at the highest level in your industry, wonderful!

But please don't do it because you think reaching that level is the only way you can be successful. Do it because it is *your* dream.

I am consistently asked what the difference is between a dream and a goal. Here's what we believe.

A dream is:

- Something deep in your heart that has been there since you were young.
- Something you would do even if you weren't getting paid for it.
- Something that has a purpose beyond yourself.

What is your dream? Write it down. Don't worry though, sometimes we can't fully articulate our dreams until we are living them.

Is that really *your* dream or is that simply how you define success in your profession, education, sport, or relationship?

-CHAPTER-

Moving From *What If* To <u>Even If</u>

I wonder what would happen if we changed our "*what if* this seemingly bad thing happens" to "<u>*even if*</u> this seemingly bad thing happens."

As I was writing this chapter I was standing in a line behind at least 3,000 people waiting for a chance to buy the new iPhone 6 plus. None of us knew if they were going to have enough in stock for all of us, and it was easy to let my focus go to "what if I woke up at 4:52am to stand in line for 5 hours and NOT get a phone?!"

This type of rumination is not very helpful for peace and tranquility. It can lead to anxiety and frustration.

Here are some other examples:

- What if I treat my team with love and respect and we don't win?!
- What if I fight for my marriage for 2 years and my spouse still chooses to leave me?
- What if I give my very very best, make tons of sacrifices, and I don't make it to the league?
- What if I put people over profit and our business fails?
- What if I believe and pray for my son to be healed and he still dies at the age of 7?

Scary thoughts.

We can't control outcomes, but we do have control over a few things, and it usually works out best when we use our energy on those things.

So, I wonder what would happen if we changed our "what if's" to "even if's."

- Even if I do not get a new iPhone today, I will have an opportunity to develop more patience.
- Even if I do not make it to the league, I will know I gave it my all and will have developed characteristics that will help me in other facets of life.
- Even if my spouse chooses to leave me, I will know I did everything I could to save our marriage.
- Even if our business fails, we will have learned a lot of valuable lessons for the future.
- Even if my son dies, I will continue to trust in Jesus and believe God is good.

We don't know what you are facing or have just been through. But we have been through our share of tragedy, loss, and pain. We don't have control over what happens most of the time. However, we do have control over whether or not we ruminate on negative outcomes or we choose to look at them as, *"Even if* this happens I will not quit, I will not give in, I will persevere, I will trust, I will live a courageous life."

"Everything can be taken from a man but one thing: the last of the human freedoms—to choose one's attitude in any given set of circumstances, to choose one's own way."
Viktor Frankl –Holocaust Survivor and Author of, *Man's Search For Meaning.*

-CHAPTER-

How Are *WE* Modeling The Problem?

A person who coaches that I get to work with walked over to me and said, "What should I do if I'm not supposed to run them?! Every single one of them showed up with their shirts untucked..... I would make them run in the past, but *you say* we shouldn't use fitness as a punishment."

I looked at him and tried be as humble as possible as I said, "please look at you and your staff."

Every one of their shirts were un-tucked.

They are always learning, but we aren't always aware of what we are teaching them.

I hear people in coaching and education complaining about entitlement, awful mindset, and many other issues, but I've rarely heard them say...."**Maybe we are part of the problem.**"

John Wooden said, "Young people need models, not critics." I completely agree, and would take it one step further. *PEOPLE* need models, not critics. Anyone can be a critic, it is ridiculously hard to be a model.

TRAIN To Be Clutch

- What are your biggest challenges in the team you lead?
- In what ways could you or your support staff be modeling those problems?

Some Things I've Learned In Life

I've learned that the guy at the top of the mountain didn't fall there.

Whether it is Kobe Bryant, Tiger Woods, Lebron James, or the best in any business, when you get behind the scenes it becomes very obvious why they became the best in the world.

I've learned by spending at least 10 minutes in gratefulness prayer at the beginning of my day thanking God for everything in my life, my days go much better.

I've learned the good and the bad are always available for me to focus on. And since I had no problem ignoring the good for so many years in my life, I don't mind ignoring the bad now.

I've learned I would rather inspire people to greatness than strike fear in them with control tactics.

I've learned there is no such thing as a realist, and we live our lives based on our perception of reality, which is greatly complicated by a myriad of factors. Mainly by only being aware of around .0001% of what our brains are processing per second, and secondly by creating the world around us by our beliefs.

I've learned that rather than asking God to change my circumstances I would much prefer to read His word and let it change how I think.

I've learned people are infatuated with success, but they get scared when they see what it actually takes to get there.

I've learned if you only put in what you think they deserve, you will rarely have a great experience and you will never achieve your greatest potential.

I've learned the tough circumstances in life make the good times so much more meaningful. I thank God for a warm bed everyday because I know what it's like to sleep on concrete.

I've learned I don't want to wait until I have cancer to appreciate EVERYTHING in my life. Even the little things like clean drinking water.

I've learned I rarely have control over my circumstances, but I always have control over the explanation of what those circumstances mean to me.

I've learned even though it feels like the sun revolves around us, the sun actually never moves and we revolve around the SON.

I've learned regardless of my circumstances I always have the opportunity to love, serve, provide value, and I have control over my attitude, effort, self-talk, perspective, and how I carry myself.

I've learned my dreams are usually on the other side of whatever problems keep arising in my life, and that through a willingness to tackle those challenges I grow into the person I want to become.

I've learned that my work ethic and willingness to sacrifice must be greater than my dreams.

I've learned if I am not content with what I have, then I won't be content with what I get.

I've learned the harder I train, the more willing I am to sacrifice, the more I treat people well, the more I persist, the more I use proven strategies, the more open I am to growth, the "luckier" I get.

I've learned if I put the wrong fuel in my heart that I will get stuck and that I have to be my own best coach.

I've learned until you take yourself seriously no one else will take you seriously either.

I've learned love is stronger than hate.

I've learned it really does take a bigger person to overcome evil with good.

I've learned by focusing on becoming the best I can be and taking advantages of the small opportunities in my hand that new opportunities naturally will come to me.

I've learned it always seems impossible until someone does it.

I've learned what I believe about myself greatly impacts my future reality.

I've learned since I live in the United States I'm never missing resources, only resourcefulness.

I've learned giving your very best is a much higher standard than winning. Anyone can win, but very few can consistently give their very best.

I've learned the most successful people I know embrace adversity.

I've learned no matter who you are or how talented you think you are, you can never skip plateaus. You can only embrace them as a part of the journey to the elusive concept of mastery.

I've learned everyone has brilliant ideas, but VERY VERY few are willing to sacrifice, work, and persist to transform those ideas to practical, viable solutions.

I've learned the path to sustained excellence is always paved with failure, so I might as well embrace it.

I've learned to be excited when things are tough and when I go through hard times because those hard times help me become even better, and they make for the best stories.

I've learned if I'm going to do something, I might as well give my very best. I'm already in it, so I might as well embrace it and get something great out of it.

I've learned to spend all my energy on things inside of my control.

I've learned to become so good they can't ignore you.

I've learned that time is way more valuable than money. You can get more money, but you can never get more time.

I've learned if you fail to take advantage of the small opportunities right in front of you, you won't be prepared for the opportunities of your dreams.

I've learned there is nothing I'm going through that someone else hasn't been through, made it through, and then written about their experience.

I've learned success always looks easy when you haven't been around to see how hard someone has worked for it.

I've learned if you really want something as bad as you say you do then your life would look radically different because you would make different daily choices.

I've learned "limits like fears are often just an illusion"- Michael Jordan

I learned from John Maxwell that my dreams are outside of my comfort zone, and that to achieve them I must become comfortable with being uncomfortable.

I've learned that intelligent persistence is a trait of all world changers.

I've learned the 4 things that actually determine how I feel are:
1.) What I focus on
2.) My perspective
3.) My body language
4.) My self-talk

I've learned that passion, patience, and persistence will help you succeed EVEN with poor strategies.

I've learned the fastest way to get to places beyond your wildest dreams is to become the very best you can be, right where you are, with what you've got.

I've learned that the best rarely got that way with the best equipment and resources.

I've learned that most great things come from experiments, not theories.

I've learned that every storm eventually runs out of rain.

I've learned Wisdom + Focused Effort + Persistence = Brilliant Results

I've learned to believe in the possibility that it could happen, and then keep working until it does.

I've learned to stop hating on myself by wasting time, not taking advantage of everything in my hand, surrounding myself with negative influences, treating people poorly, and having a poor attitude.

I've learned that forgiveness is about me and not the other person. If I don't forgive them it's like I'm swallowing poison and expecting them to die from it.

I've learned to stay hungry, to stop looking at what I don't have, and start being extremely grateful for what I do have.

I've learned at some point YOU have to want it so bad YOU are willing to make the sacrifices and push through obstacles. Mentors help, but it's ultimately up to you.

I've learned when I put first things first, that like C.S. Lewis said, second things are not suppressed but they increase.

I've learned to try and take advantage of the 86,400 seconds everyday as if I were going to get the opportunity of my dreams.

I've learned to not follow my dreams, but to chase them with everything I have.

I've learned employers aren't looking for people who want a paycheck; they are looking for people who share a similar passion and who want to partner with them to achieve it.

I've learned if I can do all the little things 5-15% better than everyone else, that I would become one of the best in the world at what I do.

I learned from Jon Gordon that the difference between an average Major Leaguer and a Hall of Famer is a measly 1.7 hits per week.

I've learned true desire, much like belief, is most accurately measured by actions. Show me what you do with your time and I'll show you how bad you want it.

I've learned what got me to this level will rarely get me to the next level, and that the toll way to greatness is a very costly road.

I've learned from Sun Tzu that "every battle is won (or lost) before it's ever fought. It's in the mind.

I've learned that the things that will have the greatest influence on where I will be in five years are: what I read, who I surround myself with, what I listen to, what I watch, what I say to myself, and what I see in my head.

MORE TOOLS

Creating A Performance Cue Card

One alternative to goal setting we share with people is what we call a performance cue card. Our performance cue card is a very useful tool for us on the journey.

It looks like this:

At the top of the card you have your mission or vision for you life.

Example 1: To make people feel unconditionally loved and valued for who they are as people.

Example 2: To train and equip athletes for life after college.

Example 3: To become the best I am capable of being. A person who exhibits true mental toughness and who is a role model for young people all over the world.

Example 4: My mission for my life is to love people unconditionally and pursue excellence in everything I do. My mission for myself in my craft is to become the most mentally tough person I can be, focusing on having a great attitude, giving my very very best, treating people really really well, and having unconditional gratitude regardless of my circumstances.

The point is not for us to tell you what to write, but for you to answer these questions:

What is the mission for my life? What is my mission in sport? What is my mission in coaching? What is my mission serving as the president of this company? What is my mission as a parent? Etc...

On the left hand side of the card, and under the vision, we write out a list of 100% controllable keys to success.

Example 1: Person who coaches
100% controllable keys to success:
    1.) Smile
    2.) Breathe
    3.) Powerful body language
    4.) Talk to myself vs. listen to myself
    5.) Encourage what I want to see more of

Example 2: Person who plays golf
100% controllable keys to success:

1.) Not breaking my wrist through take away.
2.) Keep my head down through putts.
3.) Good pace regardless of my scores.
4.) Smile
5.) Focused on process not results
6.) Focused on one shot at a time

Example 3: Person who plays basketball
100% controllable keys to success:
1.) Fake a pass to make a pass
2.) Play present at all times
3.) Stay low and in a stance
4.) Over communicate at all times
5.) Enjoy the journey
6.) Encourage my teammates

Example 4: Person in business
100% controllable keys to success:
1.) Smile
2.) Breathe
3.) Powerful body language
4.) Talk to myself vs. listen to myself
5.) Encourage what I want to see more of

Now directly across from the keys to success, on the right side of the page, we will have our beneficial and constructive self-talk statements.

Example 1: Person who coaches
Beneficial and Constructive Self-Talk Statements
1.) Whatever happens to me is in my best interest and can be an opportunity to learn and grow.
2.) Coach Present
3.) Don't let them see you sweat!

4.) Breathe and let it go.

5.) The next opportunity I can _____.

6.) At least I have access to clean drinking water.

Example 2: Person who plays golf

Beneficial and Constructive Self-Talk Statements

1.) Whatever happens to me is in my best interest and can be an opportunity to learn and grow.

2.) Play Present

3.) Enjoy this moment, because one day you will want to be back here no matter how it feels now!

4.) I'm just getting warmed up.

5.) Breathe and let it go.

6.) The next opportunity I can _____.

7.) At least I have access to clean drinking water.

Example 3: Person who plays basketball

Beneficial and Constructive Self-Talk Statements

1.) Whatever happens to me is in my best interest and can be an opportunity to learn and grow.

2.) Play Present.

3.) Next Play.

4.) I'm just getting warmed up.

5.) Breathe and let it go.

Example 4: Person in business

Beneficial and Constructive Self-Talk Statements

1.) Whatever happens to me is in my best interest and can be an opportunity to learn and grow.

2.) Be here now

3.) Breathe and let it go.

4.) Right now I can _____.

5.) At least I have access to clean drinking water.

Now in the bottom left hand corner of our card we will write down a time when we felt extremely confident. It doesn't have to be in the same field as you are creating the performance card for. For example, it could be a 7th grade violin recital even though you are a making your card for football. It just needs to be a time that you can remember performing at your very best and when you were extremely confident.

Next to that we are going put a picture of something that helps us regain a healthy perspective. This could be a picture of our family, a special place like Hawaii, a family pet, or anything that will help you regain a healthy perspective. However, we do not recommend you have a picture of your boyfriend or girlfriend. Hawaii is most likely going to be around in 20 years, but the boyfriend or girlfriend may not be.

Next to the picture we are going to write down our peak performance number from 1-10. Sometimes this is referred to as our optimum arousal state. Think about 1 being very steady and methodical, showing almost no emotion regardless of circumstance. Think about 10 being extremely high energy and much more emotional. When do you perform at your very best?

I wish I had learned about this when I was younger. My number for sports is probably a 6 or a 7, however, I always tried to get myself up to a 9 or 10. This is just what I thought you were supposed to do before games! I would listen to rap music, watch movies like *Braveheart*, or *Man on Fire*, in order to get pumped up. This worked fine during games where I needed that extra energy, but in big games it often backfired. I got too high, and I often got kicked out of games because I was operating in the red. Much like a car, with the rpm's operating in the red, I would overheat and have some type of explosion. For example, in undergrad we were playing the 19th ranked team in the country and I scored two goals against them before I was ejected from the game for a reckless tackle.

You may not know what your peak performance number is, and that is ok. You need to ask other people when they think you play at your best, and then start to pay more attention until you start to figure it out. This could take a few weeks. You might also need to have different numbers for different parts of the game, round of golf, or parts of your day. Maybe you need to start at a five, then get to an eight, but then get down to a three when you are closing things out. One of the most important parts is starting to understand where you want to get to so you can manipulate your energy levels. If we need to lower our number we can do deep breathing exercises and listen to classical music to lower our heart rate and get to a lower number. If we need to get to a higher number we can jump around, and repeat some intense beneficial and constructive self-talk to get our number higher. Before a competition we can listen to up-beat music, watch inspirational media, and jump around to get our number higher.

From our experience, many times it is the game against the perceived weaker opponent when we need to manufacture our levels to a higher state. Most of the time when we are performing in a "BIG" game, the best thing we can do is actually put things back into perspective and make sure we are listening and watching things that calm us down, not hype us up.

The last box on the bottom right hand corner of our card is a beneficial and constructive jingle. This last year I sometimes battled with the hosel-shanks in my golf game. My jingle was, "I believe I can fly, I believe I can touch the sky." I was singing it over and over again to program my mind with what I wanted the ball to do.

Just below this section is where you will write out 2 specific areas you will direct your focus toward getting better in. These are things that you can practice and grow in no matter what the people in coaching set for your workout. Things like where you are looking, being aware of your surroundings, talking to others more, moving your feet on defense, improving your quickness, self-talk, breathing, balance, etc.

Finally, at the bottom right you will write down 1 person who you are going to make sure has a great day. Spend the whole practice and game making sure to give them appropriate encouragement and instruction. Be deliberate about giving them high fives and chest bumps. Make sure that you do everything in your power to make sure they grow that day.

Here is an example of what a completed card could look like.

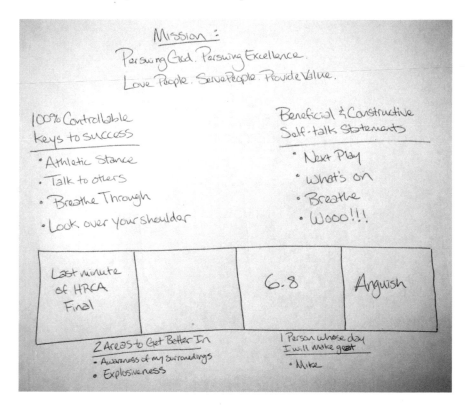

Mission- My mission for my life is to become the type of person who pursues excellence with passion in everything I do. My mission is to serve the needs of the sick. My mission for myself in my craft is to exhibit true mental toughness to the best of my ability. My mission is to be an ambassador of the game, and a role model for kids in the community.

100% Controlllable Keys To Success	Beneficial and Constructive Self-Talk Statements
1.) Fake a pass to make a pass	-"Breath and let it go"
2.) Play present at all times	-"You can get the next one"
3.) Stay low and in a stance	-"It is in my best interest"
4.) Over communicate at all times	-"The tough stuff only makes me stronger"
5.) Enjoy the journey	-"Play present"
6.) Encourage my teammates	

Game against Arizona

When I had a triple double.   My peak performance is a 7.   "I believe I can fly."

Before performance :

Re-write EVERYTHING from performance cue card onto a sheet of paper.

Mission
100% controllable keys to success
Beneficial Self-talk statements
Most confident performance
Peak performance number
Beneficial jingle
Two ways to improve
One person whose day you will make great

On the back of the performance cue card we will do the Dispute Negative Thinking exercise.

Write out 2-4 of the gremlins (negative beliefs/thoughts) that pop up into your mind when you are performing. Then act like a good attorney and write out the hard evidence to the contrary.

For example:

Negative belief "I'm not good enough to play at this level"
Hard evidence:
- As a person playing D-1 athletics I am in the top .00001% of all people playing golf who started playing when we were younger.
- I placed in the top 10 at the Palos Verdes tournament
- I was recruited to play here

Negative belief "I suck at putting"
Hard evidence:
- At the Alabama tournament I finished a round with 28 putts
- Last year I dropped 2 putts off my average putts per round
- At Augusta last year I finished a round with 29 putts

Our best advice is to write out your card every single day until it becomes so engrained in your daily thought process it is almost completely natural to you.

What Went Well Journals

No single exercise has been more effective for the people we train than the "what went well" journaling every day. Our memories are recreated through the retelling of events, so writing out what went well during practice, meetings, games, tournaments, or any other event impacts what we remember about the event. By consistently completing your what went well journal you will train your brain to scan the world for what has gone well instead of the few things that were less than perfect.

At the top you write out: "My value comes from who I am, not from what I do."

Write out 15-63 specific things that went well. This will be incredibly hard at first because you are literally retraining the way your brain sees the world. Keep going! It will get easier as you continue to complete the exercise.

Write out 2 areas for growth.

Write out 2 things you learned.

Example: (I am using varied examples from different contexts.)

"My value comes from who I am and NOT what I do."

What Went Well
1.) After hitting a poor shot on #2 I used beneficial and constructive self-talk.
2.) I had great body language for the first part of the game.
3.) I communicated loud and often with my teammates.
4.) During the business meeting when Jon was using poor language, I chose to focus on what I could control.
5.) I finished through contact and made my free throw.
6.) I carried myself with powerful body language even after hitting a bad shot on #7.
7.) I treated my teammates very well even though I didn't play as well as I would have liked.
8.) I hit a great pitch shot on #9.
9.) Even when my son was acting poorly, I still treated him with love and respect, and enforced healthy boundaries.
10.) I had a great attitude all day, even though I didn't play to the best of my abilities.
11.) I chose to talk to myself rather than listen to myself even when things got tough during competition.
12.) I looked the person coaching me in the eye even when she was telling me things I didn't agree with.
13.) I hit a great putt on #18.
14.) I made a great pass to Jacob to create a scoring opportunity.
15.) I took a great shot in the first half and the goalie made a great save.

Areas For Growth
1.) I need to grow in the area of my short game shots.
2.) I need to grow in my patience when losing.

Things I Learned
1.) I learned I play much better if I stay down in a defensive stance and I communicate with my teammates.
2.) I learned my iron shots go a little bit farther toward the ends of my rounds when I am excited.

Train To Be CLUTCH Challenge

The challenge is to commit to reading each of these books in two weeks, and in one year you will have read at least 28 books. The second part of the challenge is to either write a 5-page synopsis of the books with your favorite quotes and stories of what you learned and how it can benefit you as a coach, and your players, OR to transcribe your highlights into a word document to have to review, and or, send to people as a tool.

If you complete this challenge you will transform as a leader in the most powerful ways, and you will be modeling one of the most beneficial activities for those you lead. I believe the best leaders are voracious readers, and these are the books from which the Train to be CLUTCH philosophies have been built around. The only book that isn't listed is the Bible, which I believe is the foundation from which all the other wisdom flows.

If you take on the challenge, I will answer 2-3 questions per book as long as you stay on pace with the challenge. If you are interested, please sign and send back your commitment letter.

1. Mindset, by Carol Dweck
2. Burn Your Goals, by Joshua Medcalf and Jamie Gilbert
3. The Only Way to Win, by Jim Loehr
4. In a pit with a lion on a snowy day, by Mark Batterson
5. How to Stop the Pain, by Dr. James Richards
6. Mind Gym, by Gary Mack
7. Inside out Coaching, by Joe Ehrmann

8. Life is _____. By Judah Smith
9. The Promise of a Pencil, by Adam Braun
10. Wooden on Leadership, by John Wooden
11. Think and Grow Rich a Black Choice, by Dennis Kimbro
12. Leadership and Self Deception, by the Arbinger Institute
13. Unbroken, by Laura Hillenbrand
14. Before Happiness, by Shawn Anchor
15. Boundaries, by Cloud and Townsend
16. The Talent Code, by Daniel Coyle
17. Gifted Hands, by Ben Carson
18. How children succeed, by Paul Tough
19. Unconditional Parenting, by Alfie Kohn
20. Talent is Overrated, by Geoff Colvin
21. Power Relationships, by Andrew Sobel
22. Choke, by Sian Beilock
23. Question behind the question, by John Miller
24. Power Questions, Andrew Sobel and Jerold Panas
25. Drive, by Daniel Pink
26. 12 Huge Mistakes Parents Can Avoid, by Tim Elmore
27. The Carpenter, by Jon Gordon
28. Learned Optimism, by Martin Seligman
29. Mastery, by George Leonard
30. More Than A Carpenter, by Josh McDowell
31. 177 Mental Toughness Secrets of the World Class
32. Awaken The Giant Within, by Tony Robbins
33. Ten Minute Toughness, by Jason Selk
34. Obliquity, by John Kay
35. Unprofessional, by Jack Delosa
36. Toughness, by Jay Bilas
37. The Anatomy of Peace, by the Arbinger Institute
38. The Energy Bus, by Jon Gordon
39. Training Camp, by Jon Gordon
40. Jesus Is _____?, by Judah Smith
41. The Man Watching, by Tim Crothers
42. Wild Goose Chase, by Mark Batterson
43. Your Best Just Got Better, by Jason Womack

44. Overcoming the dark side of leadership, by Mcintosh & Rima
45. Eat to Live, by Joel Fuhrman
46. The Monk Who Sold His Ferrari, by Robin Sharma
47. A Team of Rivals
48. Long Walk To Freedom
49. Positivity, by Barbara Fredrickson

I _____ commit to the Train to be CLUTCH Leaders Challenge of reading the books IN ORDER listed in the challenge. I understand this is a full one to two year commitment I am making to read and write about all the books on the list.

Date- _____

Printed Name- _____

Signed Name- _____

Please scan and email Joshua@traintobeclutch.com

Thank YOU'S From Joshua

To everyone who has played a role in my life over the last 29 years, thank you!

I'm incredibly grateful to my mother who has supported me and been one of my best friends my whole life. Thank you for never giving up on me when no one would have blamed you if you had.

Thank you to my father who did the best he could with what he had.

Thank you to Tim McClements for never giving up on me at Vanderbilt and helping me get a scholarship at Duke. I was a royal pain in your ass, and I'm forever grateful you stuck by my side.

I'm so grateful to Jamie and Amy, you both have been such an amazing support system in my life, and I'm so grateful I get to spend so much time with you.

Thank you Amber for always listening to my stories. Hopefully one day you will learn something from them.

Thank you to Austin, TJ, Kyle, Joe, Pooter, Krause, Brady, Tim, and my many other friends who have been there for me during the many low points in my life.

Thank you Anson for all your words of encouragement and allowing me to work with your program.

Thank you Danny and Ryan for always praying for me and being great friends in LA. You both have taught me so much about Jesus and how to love people more.

Thank you Judah Smith for being the most amazing pastor a person could ask for. You have taught me so much about Jesus, how He really feels about me, and how I can live like Him. I don't think anyone has ever had such a profound impact on my life in such a short period of time as you have.

Thank you Lisa for always being there to hear my articles, or just to listen to another one of my crazy stories.

Thank you Cori for taking a chance on me and giving me the opportunity to work with your amazing program.

Thank you Ria for being such an inspiration in my life and being one of my favorite people in the whole world.

Thank you Kelia for showing me how powerful a smile and warm presence can be in the world.

Thank you Russ and Skip for all the mentorship over the years. Thank you Skip for being one of the first people outside of my family to financially invest in me and my dreams.

Thank you Jan, Drew, Jim, for enduring and editing early drafts with my very poor grammar. Thank you Thom for all the edits for the second version of this book!

Thank you Andy and Terry for teaching me so much as a teenager. I wouldn't be here today without your love and wisdom.

Thank you Adri for all your prayers and friendship.

Thank you Jesus for your extravagant and undeserved love.

Thank You's From Jamie

I truly believe that there are hundreds of thousands of people who have influenced my life and the way I think. So to everyone I've connected with, thank you.

More specifically, I want to thank my wife Amy. Your passion for Christ, people, and life inspires me every day. Thank you for loving Jesus more than you love me and for being my unconditional smile and support in everything. You are the cheese to my macaroni!

To my son, James, your smile and voice make me melt every single day! Chase your dreams!

To my parents, Karen and Lawrence, thank you for your unconditional love. I cannot find one memory where you made me feel like my worth came from anything I did or did not do.
Thank you for your commitment to Jesus and the marriage and lives you have modeled. Your love and support has allowed us to faithfully pursue the dreams we believe God has placed in our heart!

To Jim and Katie, thank you for allowing me to be a part of your family. You have loved me unconditionally and we thank you for your continual love and support in pursuit of our passions.

To Joey Ryan, thank you for your wisdom and leadership both in soccer and in life.

To Tim Lonergan, your faithfulness to Christ and compassion as a friend sparked the transformation of my heart and mind. No doubt, it is having an eternal impact on hundreds of thousands of people across the world!

To Tony and Leslie Coffey, thank you for your mentorship, friendship, and delicious desserts.

To Annette and Richie Grant, thank you for taking me in and feeding me as though I was one of your own.

To Dan, Amy, Johno, Lisa, Jane, Gary, John, and all of our family in Ballymun, thank you for the laughs, the love, and the many cups of tea.

To everyone at the Irish Bible Institute, thank you for your passion and commitment to Christ.

To Tim McClements and Richie Grant, thank you for training me in soccer and in life.

To Steve, thank you for taking a chance on me at the Rapids.

To Wenmi and Duncan, thanks for providing me work, love, and plenty of life lessons.

To Casey McQuillan, cheers for everything! I mean everything!

To Cheryl, Bart, Ty, TK, and Hiedi, thank you for allowing me to be a part of your lives and for providing the training ground that has influenced tens of thousands.

To Joshua, thank you for being a wonderful friend all of these years. I don't know who we'd be or what we'd be doing if you hadn't interceded. Thank you for your vision, passion, and willingness to learn and grow. Without you life would be a little less crazy and lot more boring!

To God, thank you for your grace and faithfulness. You're right: My ways are not your ways. You truly are the God of Enough!